SERMONS IN STONE

COUNTRYMAN PRESS
An imprint of W.W. Norton & Company
Independent Publishers Since 1923

SERMONS IN STONE

THE STONE WALLS OF
NEW ENGLAND AND NEW YORK

BY

SUSAN ALLPORT

ILLUSTRATED BY

DAVID HOWELL

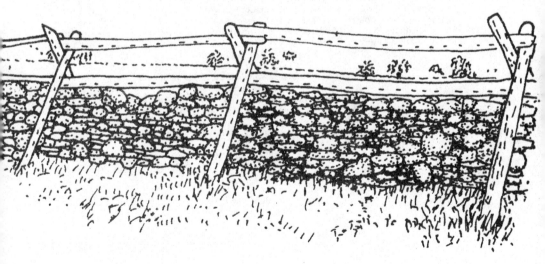

To
MARGARET NOYES HOWELL
whose love of books
inspired
even a dyslexic

Copyright © 1990, 2012 by Susan Allport

First published as a W. W. Norton paperback 1994
First published as a Countryman Press paperback 2012

For information about permission to reproduce selections from this book, write
to Permissions, Countryman Press, 500 Fifth Avenue, New York, NY 10110

For information about special discounts for bulk purchases, please contact
W. W. Norton Special Sales at specialsales@wwnorton.com or 800-233-4830

Excerpts from "Mending Walls" and "Of the Stones of the Place" are from *The Poetry of Robert Frost*, edited by Edward Connery Lathem. Copyright 1930, 1939, © 1969 by Holt, Rinehart and Winston. Copyright 1942, 1958 by Robert Frost. Copyright © 1967, 1970 by Lesley Frost Ballantine. Reprinted by permission of Henry Holt and Company, Inc. Excerpts on pages 117-118 are from *Yankee Drover: Being the Unpretending Life of Asa Sheldon, Farmer, Trader, and Working Man, 1788-1870*. John Seelye, fwd. © 1988 by University Press of New England.

Library of Congress Cataloging in Publication Data
Allport, Susan
Sermons in stone : the stone walls of New England and
New York / by Susan Allport ; illustrated by David Howell.
p.   cm.
1. Stone walls—New England.   2. Stone walls—New York (State).
I. Title.
NA2940.A45   1990
725' .96' 0974—dc20   89–49372
ISBN 978-1-58157-165-3

Countryman Press
www.countrymanpress.com

An imprint of W. W. Norton & Company, Inc.,
500 Fifth Avenue, New York, NY 10110
www.wwnorton.com

1 0 9 8 7 6 5

ACKNOWLEDGMENTS

THIS book would not have been possible without the generous assistance of many of the many historians, curators, and librarians who willingly searched their files and collections for the odd piece of inforation relating to stone walls. It would be very difficult to name them all, but we are particularly indebted to Elizabeth Fuller at the library of the Westechester County Historical Society; John Herzan of the connecticut Historical Commission; Elizabeth Knox of the new London County Historical Society; Richard Landaers, town historian of Northcastle; Rosemary Mahone, secretary to the Bedford Town Historian; Diane Norman of the Otis Library; Mary Baker Wood of Old Sturbridge Village; Andrew Vadnais at the Mount Lebanon Shaker Village; Virginia Fetscher at the Katonah Villiage Library (who never failed to obtain even the most obscure volumes); and Amy Barnum at the New York State Historical Association Library in Cooperstown. We'd also like to express appreciation to those who gave their time to be interviewed for this project, including among others, Shirley Albright, Richard Lasher, Eldress Bertha Lindsey, Barbara Narenda, Drew Outhouse, Derek Owen, Walter and Mary Plant, Mitchell Poisin, Roslyn Strong, and Iren Zegarelli; and to those who read and commented on the book in its various stages: Lou Raymond, Andrew Vadnais, Sarah Clayton, Barbara Mayer, and Giovanna Peebles. Andy Marasia, Deborah Hoyt, Holly Yakman, and Rebecca Castillo took on the unusual demands of this project with cheerful equanimity.

We'd like to give special thanks to our daughters, Liberty and Cecil, who good-humoredly accompanied us on many wall-watching trips (thinly disguised as family vacations), and to Rachael Peden, Nancy Palmquist, and Mary Cunnane for their invaluable pictorial and editorial advice.

S. A. and D. H.

CONTENTS

PART IV THE WALLS OF AFFLUENCE

Preface to the New Edition

Twenty-five years or so ago, when I first began to entertain the notion of writing a book on stone walls, I had no idea what I was going to find. The idea was actually my husband's, and when he suggested it, I was extremely dubious. I was a science writer, after all, and doubted that there was enough meat on a stone wall's bones, so to speak, to build a book around.

I was really stepping into the unknown. So little had been written about stone walls, I was worried that it would turn out there was very little to write. I worried that I would commit myself to the project, find nothing, then wind up writing a light and frothy book—my particular secret dread.

But all the time I was debating whether or not to write on this subject, I was intrigued by a central contradiction: On one hand, stone walls are everywhere, endless. On the other, so little was known about them. Like many of us, I sensed that these walls must have stories to tell, but for the moment, although they were everywhere, they were mute. Evocative but silent.

I knew, of course, that they were a part of New York and New England's agricultural past—the ruins of that past, so to speak—but surely their history didn't begin and end there. Who had built these walls and why? Did they just mark property lines, as is so often said? Or were these tumbling-down structures once effective barriers for cows and sheep? And how did the people who built these walls view their labors? How did they see the stones they removed from their fields? Where did they think those stones had come from? Were stone walls a good kind of fence or something the farmers of this area just had to make do with? Could anyone build a stone wall or was it a task that you had to have a particular knack or talent for?

In order to learn the answers to these questions, I knew I would have to cast a very wide net. Once I'd decided to go ahead with the project, I wrote to hundreds of historical societies and libraries asking if they had any information regarding stone walls. (These were the days before the Internet, of course, and all this took a great deal of time, paper, and stamps.) Considering the quantity of wall that existed where each of these libraries was located, it was amazing that most wrote back saying they had nothing whatsoever on the subject. Some, however, sent small but tantalizing tidbits.

The Little Compton Historical Society in Rhode Island, for example, sent an excerpt from the town records of Plymouth from 1672 in which an Indian squaw was given a fine of building twenty poles of stone wall as partial payment for a 25-pound debt she owed one John Almy. (A pole or a rod, by the way, is a unit of measurement equivalent to 16½ feet.)

A North Salem historian gave me a page from the account books of one of her ancestors on which it was noted that in 1787 a slave named Robbin was given a credit of 32 shillings for "Making stone fence and for four days carting stone."

The New Haven Historical Society sent a page from the court records of 1653 in which the settlers of New Haven promised to build a fence around the corn fields of the local Indians. In return, the Indians pledged to "doe no damage to the English Cattell and to secure their owne corne from damage [sic]." These are just a few examples. It was not a lot of material, but it was enough to start shaking my preconceptions about stone walls and send me digging in many different, profitable directions.

I started out thinking of stone walls simply as picturesque byproducts of our agricultural past, as inextricably tied to the Yankee farmer and his labors as an ox to a plow. But with each new piece of information, I came to see that they were much more complex objects with a much more complex past. That they had been built by slaves and Indians as well as Yankees, that their very existence was due as much to deforestation during the colonial period as it was to the amount of stone dumped on the area by the glaciers thousands of years ago.

In the decades since *Sermons in Stone* was first published, my husband and I have seen a great growth of interest in stone walls—in both their history and their preservation. We like to think our book has played some part in this and that it will continue to generate interest in these walls and surprise readers with how much they have to say.

Susan Allport
David Howell
Katonah, New York
April 28, 2012

"Good and secure fences are better than a hot toddy, or all the soporific drugs of Turkey or Arabia, to sleep upon; you not only know where your cattle are, but where they are not."

Rural New Yorker, 1856

"Sweet are the uses of adversity,
Which, like the toad, ugly and venomous,
Wears yet a precious jewel in his head;
And this our life, exempt from public haunt,
Finds tongues in trees, books in the running brooks,
Sermons in stones, and good in every thing."

As You Like It, Act II, Scene I

PART I

GENERATIONS OF FENCES

1

THE RUINS OF NEW ENGLAND

THERE is a drama in the woods of New England and southern New York that may not be found anywhere else in the world. This is a drama that comes not just from the physical beauty of this part of the world, though that is considerable: a seemingly endless repetition of narrow valleys and steep hills punctuated by enormous rock outcroppings that rise from the floor of the young forests like great gray whales surfacing for air. Nor does it come from the possibility—so eagerly embraced when walking in the woods—that you are walking where no man or woman has walked before. Strangely enough, it arises instead out of this possibility's exact opposite: the sure knowledge that someone *has* walked here before, and most likely in the company of an ox or a plow.

For in the woods of New England are the ruins of this area's agricultural past, the remains of eighteenth-, nineteenth-, even twentieth-century farms, farms abandoned so recently that it is amazing how little evidence of them still exists. Their fields have returned to forest; their barns and houses have rotted. Indeed, almost all that is left are the stone structures: foundations, old wells, and mile after mile of stone walls, crisscrossing the land, marking old boundaries and pastures, delineating cow runs, and climbing the sides of the steepest hills.

But what this evidence lacks in kind—or diversity—it makes up in quantity. These walls seem endless. They speak, of course, of how extensively New England was once cultivated, that 150 years ago, seventy-five to eighty percent of the area was cleared and farmed. They speak also of how quickly the past is forgotten. Today, when so much is said about protecting the small family farms of the West and Midwest, we barely remember that New England too was a region of small family farms—in 1850, 168,000 of them—abandoned when the various forces of railroad expansion, Western competition, soil exhaustion, farm mechanization, and government price supports made them unprofitable to run. Hikers come across stone walls in the woods and

The view from the Tea House in North Salem, New York, as it looked in the early 1900s. In the nineteenth and early twentieth centuries, visitors flocked to this restaurant to enjoy vistas of fields, fences, and, on a clear day, Long Island Sound. In the last seventy or eighty years, however, those vistas have disappeared. As in other parts of New England and New York, some seventy-five percent of the land that was once under cultivation has been left to revert back to forest; and today, looking out from the site where the Tea House once stood, you can see nothing but trees.

they are surprised, puzzled until they dig back in their minds for the key that opens the lock of these mysterious works of backbreaking effort, as out of place and evocative as a shipwreck on the ocean floor. This was where the country began, in these woods, and in agriculture, not industry.

Written in these walls are eloquent reminders of the odds against which the early farmers of this area worked, tilling thinly soiled ground whose main claim to fecundity was the abundant crop of rock that heaved to the surface each winter. There are reminders too of our own mortality: that rough wall over there may be all that remains of one man's labors. And yet in this age of planned obsolescence, that shiver of a thought must be closely followed by another: "My God, how that wall endures!" There is not a sign of the house and barns that would make sense of this sprawl of rocks on rock, yet that wall is still there to say that these woods were not always so, that they once were fields, and that the walls enclosed not young birches and shaggy-bark hickories but cows and crops.

NOBODY KNOWS HOW many miles of stone walls there are in New England and New York today, but a 1871 Department of Agriculture report, *Statistics of Fences in the United States*, gives us a very good idea of how many existed about a hundred years ago. The survey was made during a period when a nationwide shortage of fencing materials threatened to curb Western expansion. The value of a farmer's fences was often greater than that of the cattle, crops, and land they enclosed, and some Americans were beginning to feel that much of the nation's fencing was unnecessary and that fence laws placed too much of a burden on those who planted crops and not enough on cattle owners. It was also a time when the widespread deforestation of New England had turned field stone—long the bane of a farmer's existence—into a valuable natural asset.

The results of the survey are astounding. In 1871 approximately one-third of Connecticut's fences were made of stone, amounting to 20,505 miles of stone wall—enough to extend almost one time around the equator. Most of Rhode Island's 14,030 miles of fencing were stone, as were nearly half of Massachusetts: 32,960 miles. In New York, eighteen percent of the fences were made of stone, a staggering 95,364 miles, more miles than there are in the coastline of the entire United States. Taken together, the states of New England and New York had more miles of stone walls than the United States has miles of railroad track today. The work that went into them, according to one estimate, would have built the pyramids of Egypt one hundred times over.

When the naturalist Edwin Way Teale bought a farm in a northern section of Connecticut in 1959, he was awestruck by the walls (many of which were chest or shoulder high and up to six feet wide) that divided and subdivided his 130 acres. So one day he attached a pedometer to his belt and walked the length of every wall. The extent of these walls—the walls of one, average-sized farm in Connecticut—was five miles, a testimony both to the amount of stone the glaciers dumped on Teale's land and to the men who removed it. It has been said that two men could build about ten feet of stone wall a day, an estimate that included the time required to gather the stones and lay a foundation. At that rate it would have taken two men about seven full years to lay the walls on Teale's farm. It would have taken 1,000 men working 365 days a year about 59 years to build all the stone walls of Connecticut and 15,000 men 243 years to build the 252,539 miles of walls in New England and New York.

Another informal survey dates back to 1746 when Thomas Church, a representative from what was then Little Compton, Massachusetts, told his fellow representatives that his town had enough stone wall to reach from Little Compton to Boston, a distance of some seventy-four miles. The other representatives refused to believe him, and Church returned home to check his facts. At the next session of the General Court, he announced that he had been in error: there was enough stone wall to reach from Little Compton to Boston —and back again.

In other parts of the United States, stone was also used as a fencing material, though not nearly as extensively as in New England and New York. In the 1871 survey, stone walls were reported in Maryland, North Carolina, South Carolina, West Virginia, Tennessee, Ohio, Michigan, Wisconsin, Kansas, Pennsylvania, and New Jersey, but often in negligible quantities; either these states had enough timber to build fences of wood or they lacked the surface building stone that was so plentiful in most parts of New York and New

England. In Pennsylvania, for example, a state that is also known for its stone walls, only about four percent of the fences in 1871 were made of stone and these were concentrated in the counties of Wayne and Susquehanna. In New Jersey's northern counties, the survey noted that "a few stone walls may be seen." In North Carolina, there was "a very little of stone walls," and the county of Dickinson in Kansas reported that it had "400 rods of stone-wall [equaling 6,600 feet or a little less than a mile and a quarter], built at $2 per rod."

Not all of the walls that were reported in the Department of Agriculture's survey are still standing, of course. In the century since that survey, many of them have been destroyed. Some were buried and made into stone drains when small fields of the early New England farms were combined and enlarged. In the 1920s and 1930s, as local roads began to be paved throughout the country, many walls were turned into crushed stone and used to make macadam. Additional walls were lost when roads were widened, and many more were later dismantled to provide stone for masons who were constructing the fireplaces and foundations of innumerable rural and suburban developments.

Yet countless walls or pieces of walls still remain, winding down roads, rambling through woods, or framing the front of a house. More common than sugar maples or saltbox houses, it is difficult to imagine New England or New York without them. But who would want to? To a New Englander, other areas of the country, areas without walls, usually seem a little flat and lacking in texture. They can be beautiful, but a New Englander wonders how much more beautiful they might be with miles of walls to add scale to the landscape, as well as adding the strength of their shapes, rhythm, and color.

Everybody in New England, it seems, has their favorite. When I mention that I am writing a book on stone walls, the reaction is usually immediate and predictable. "Do you know the one on Long Ridge Road? The one with the very big cut stones?" one person will ask. "I love the one around the cemetery," another will say. A stone mason told me that I had to go and see the walls of the Shaker Village in Canterbury, New Hampshire; and a Westchester County historian volunteered that her favorite wall had just been moved—

numbered stone by numbered stone——by the town of Somers, New York, when it was enlarging its central intersection. In spite of the effort and expense that went into that move——an indication of the regard some are beginning to have for stone walls——the historian confided that she wasn't entirely pleased with the results: the new wall somehow lacked the character of the old.

As visually pleasing as stone walls are, they are much more than just aesthetic elements in the landscape. To see them only as this is to miss out on a rich tapestry of meanings that these structures have acquired over the past three centuries——and on the very different stories that these walls have to tell. Even to associate all stone walls with our early rural and agricultural past is to oversimplify things enormously. Many of the stone walls in New York and parts of New England tell stories, not of agricultural times, but of the numerous Italian immigrants who arrived in this country at the end of the nineteenth century and went to work building New York's reservoir system, the bridges and railroad beds of the Harlem River Railroad, and the homes and walls of numerous Hudson Valley, Westchester, and Connecticut estates. Italian stone masons are also responsible for the rebuilding——or relaying——of many colonial or postcolonial stone walls, especially those that dress up the front of a house.

Even those walls which do definitely date from New England's agricultural era have a very checkered past in terms of how they were regarded at different times. For much of its existence, the well-built stone wall, like carefully constructed fencing of all kinds, was looked on as an index of a good and well-ordered settlement, a measure of a farmer's worth and capabilities. In the original 1828 edition of Noah Webster's dictionary, the definition for "fence" noted that "broken windows and poor fences are evidences of idleness or poverty or both." Timothy Dwight, Yale University's itinerant president of the late eighteenth century, expressed the same commonly held opinion when he observed that "a farm well surrounded and divided by good stone walls presents to my mind, irresistibly, the image of tidy, skillful, profitable agriculture, and promises to me within doors the still more agreeable prospect of plenty and prosperity."

However, during one important period in American history, stone walls

New England's stone walls, which once enclosed cows, sheep, and pigs, look out of place in the forests that have grown up around them. These two walls, which run parallel to each other and about ten feet apart, are the remains of a cow run, the walled lane that a farmer used to herd his animals from pasture to barn and back again.

(which we view today as the most benign structures) were regarded as nothing less than a "scourge on the landscape," "an outrageous tyranny and tax," and "an eyesore that made the fields look as if they were all imprisoned." This was at the time when fencing in general had become a huge economic albatross to farmers all across the United States. But New Englanders were faced with an additional and particularly painful truth that related specifically to their stone walls. The small, walled fields that the farmers had created were impossible to adapt to the advent of horse-powered farm machinery. Such new, speedy, but often cumbersome machines as the McCormick reaper were designed to be used on the big, flat fields of the Midwest, and in New England, farmers were faced with the difficult choice of either abandoning their farms and heading West or burying their walls in order to enlarge their fields.

Even today, New England's stone walls inspire controversy and radical differences in opinion. While most historians, archaeologists, and geographers believe that these walls are firmly rooted in the traditions of colonial and postcolonial life, there are individuals who contend that certain stone walls were built by much earlier visitors from Europe—Celts or Irish monks perhaps—who, they believe, established settlements in New England more than one thousand years ago. These opposing views can make for a baffled public and somewhat humorous battles over the same turf. Friends of mine recently went on a nature walk in Ridgefield, Connecticut; when the group they were with came across a round, stone, sunken enclosure, the volunteer ranger who was leading the walk suggested that it was probably the remains of an old animal pen or cattle pound. At that, one of the other participants on the walk stepped forward to say that, no, it was definitely a celestial observatory built by Druids. Couldn't they see that it faced south, marking, therefore, the summer solstice?

The walls of New England are also the source of other disagreements and misconceptions, some of which have made it into histories of the area. The most common is that New England's stone walls were too low to be useful as fences; they served only to mark boundary lines and as a neat way of arranging stones taken out of the fields. This can be heard and read often enough to make one doubt what is patently true: the extensive historical records documenting widespread use of stone walls to enclose animals. It's easy to get to the source of this particular misconception. People see stone walls running through the woods today, and they assume that they have always run through the woods. Then they reason that one would only go to the trouble of building such a wall in order to mark a property line. What they have forgotten is that the woods were once fields and the tumbling down stone wall they see today was once a well-maintained and effective enclosure.

Another misconception has to do with the age of New England's stone walls. Looking at a stone wall today as it negotiates its way through a stand of second-growth timber, it is tempting to think that that wall has been there almost as long as farmers themselves, that the early colonists, faced with a need to fence on one hand and an abundance of rock on the other, used that rock to build their fences. Stone walls are the only fences from agricultural New England to have survived to this day, so we tend to assume that they are the only ones to have ever existed. In fact, most of New England's stone walls are relative latecomers on the landscape. It takes far longer to build a stone wall than it does to erect any other kind of fencing (rail fencing, for example), so stone walls were rarely a farmer's first solution to the problem of fencing. Those we see today are the descendants of many generations of less-hardy ancestors: fences of brush, stumps, and rails that rotted too quickly and told in the process relentless stories of the slow progress of settlements, of the difficulties of clearing heavily forested land with just an ax.

But today's misconceptions and controversies about walls take us almost to the end of the history of stone walls in New England and New York. In order to understand how these structures have acquired their varied reputations—-and to appreciate the several different waves of wall building that New England has seen, it is important to start at the beginning, before the first wall was laid.

WHEN ENGLISH AND Dutch settlers began arriving in the New World in the early 1600s, they brought with them a system of husbandry that was destined to change both the face of the land and its inhabitants. This system, radically different from that of the native Algonquin Indians, would eventually bring

Stone walls have many different tales to tell. This one at the Ward Pound Ridge Reservation in Cross River, New York, runs between a house (now the administrative offices of the Reservation) and a barn; it speaks about the realities of farm life, the difficulty of going from carriage to house without muddying one's feet. A wall must be extremely well built in order to withstand daily traffic, and this walking wall has been endowed with very large capping or top stones.

about the walling of New England and the end of the Indian way of life.

Unlike the natives of southern New England and New York who relied on a combination of hunting, gathering, and growing crops to meet their food needs, the settlers who came to the New World were determined to practice the same agronomy they had practiced in the old. Theirs was a mixed husbandry, based on raising both crops and livestock; and the boats in which they crossed the Atlantic carried the prerequisites of this system: seeds, plants, swine, goats, oxen, sheep, and cattle. But where this mixed agronomy is practiced, crops must be protected from animals; so the introduction of this new form of husbandry into the New World also meant the introduction of fencing. The "two forms of food production—animal and vegetable—are interdependent," historian Clarence Danhof explains, but "in certain respects they are also fundamentally antagonistic to one another. From this conflict necessarily follow two agricultural practices of great importance—herding and fencing."

Those of us who live surrounded by fences and walls may find it difficult to realize that fencing is not a logical consequence and necessary companion to all agriculture (the Indians of New England, who kept few domesticated animals—dogs and sometimes eagles—used fences rarely and only for fishing, hunting, and defense), but rather that it is only the sine qua non of a mixed husbandry of crops and domesticated animals. The colonists looked around at the natives' lack of enclosures and their seasonal villages and decided that the Indians "do but run over the grass, as do also the foxes and wild beasts." John Winthrop, the first governor of the Massachusetts Bay Colony and an important colonial theorist, wrote, "As for the Natives in New England, they inclose noe Land, neither have any setled habytation, nor any tame Cattle to improve the Land by, and soe have noe other but a Naturall Right to those Countries."

This "Naturall Right," Winthrop argued, was not as great as the right of the colonists. It had existed when men held the earth in common but was superseded when individuals began to grow crops, keep livestock, and improve the land by enclosing it. From such activities, Winthrop and other colonists believed, came a superior, civil right of ownership. In the Massachusetts Bay Colony, it wasn't long before these views were translated into law.

The Court of that Colony decided that "what landes any of the Indians, within this jurisdiction, have by possession or improvement, by subdueing of the same, they have the right there unto...." Thus Massachusetts Indians were granted rights to their corn fields because they had cleared them of brush and worked the land with hoes but were denied ownership of and access to the great bulk of their territory and food supplies—their clam banks, hunting lands, berry-picking areas, and fishing waters—because these were neither cultivated nor enclosed.

For their part, the colonists believed that by cultivating and enclosing the land, they were not only acquiring the means for survival but also following a biblical injunction. "Be fruitful and multiply," it is written in Genesis, "and fill the earth and subdue it...." References to "subdueing the land" appear often in colonial records and accounts. The phrase became a kind of shorthand that expressed the full range of a settler's early activities, as well as a shared belief in their benefits. To the colonists, subduing the land meant clearing the forests, draining the swamps, plowing, enclosing, and fertilizing the fields. Fencing of all kinds—including stone walls—came to be seen as an unquestionable good, proof of man's intention to improve his lot. This is not without irony, given the role that fencing in the Old World had played in the decision of at least some of these colonists to emigrate.

Most of us who know the English countryside as an irregular patchwork of hedges and fences imagine that it has always looked that way. But for the greater part of its history, England was a landscape of open fields and pastures separated by only a few fences. This system of unenclosed common fields and shared pastures (a system which depended on a plethora of shepherds and cowherds) began slowly to change in the fifteenth and sixteenth centuries as commercial agriculture developed and sheep and cattle farming expanded; it was radically transformed after 1750, when Parliament passed a number of privately sponsored Enclosure Acts giving landowners the right to enclose their portion of the common, arable land. By 1850, open fields had disappeared from all but a few villages.

When New England was first being colonized, England was still in the early phases of enclosure, but even the relatively few areas that had been enclosed were enough to demonstrate the unquestionable commercial benefits of fencing——as well as its disruptive effects. A farmer who enclosed his land was motivated to plant such new crops as turnips and clover, knowing that they would be grazed on by his livestock; and his livestock, in turn, would enrich his pastures with significantly richer manure. But fencing also reduced the demand for agricultural labor, and when common fields were enclosed and made private, many small or marginal farmers lost their grazing rights and were forced into other occupations. At least some of these displaced laborers and farmers left for the New World where they then turned around and used the natives' lack of enclosures to justify usurping their land.

The religious beliefs of the colonists played some part in this justification, but religious beliefs were often entangled with questions of self-interest. From the beginning the Dutch recognized the Indians' right to possess their land and required settlers to purchase land whenever new colonies were established. The Dutch were also tolerant and curious about the natives of New Amsterdam and had, by and large, good relations with them. The English, on the other hand, took a different tack. They claimed vast tracts of land in the name of the crown by right of discovery, and their papers and records, as if to justify their land policies, are filled with criticisms of the Indian way of life. The Puritans, whose right to the land was the most tenuous because they lacked even a royal charter to justify their settlements, were the most extreme. They tried, as historian Neal Salisbury has noted, "to transform each quest for land into a crusade against the `savage' Indians ... by defining the social and cultural differences between the two peoples in terms of religious and moral absolutes."

These absolutes left little room for the Puritans to perceive that the Algonquins of southern New England were practicing a fundamentally different, though equally valid, form of husbandry. But perhaps part of their inability to perceive this had to do with the complexity of the Indians' system of husbandry. It is, in fact, one that historians and ecologists are only now beginning to fully appreciate.

Unlike the colonial way of life, which revolved around improvement and required permanent settlements, property boundaries, and such fixed features as fences, buildings, and fields that were to be utilized year after year, the

Indian way of life was much more mobile. The Indians of New England had learned to exploit the seasonal diversity of their environment—spring's fish spawnings, summer's abundance of fruits and forage plants, fall's exceptional hunting. And instead of permanence, this way of life demanded mobility and a certain transience—transient corn fields which were to be abandoned once they had lost their fertility, transient villages and hunting and fishing camps (which, however, were permanent in a larger sense since the same groups of Indians returned to them year after year). It also required a commitment to the nonaccumulation of property, to owning little that could not be carried on their backs. The colonists could not understand why Indians lived like paupers in a land of plenty because they were unable to comprehend this more peripatetic way of life.

The colonists also had many misconceptions about Indian division of labor. They tended to admire Indian women, whose job (like that of the white males) was to work the corn fields, but they had nothing but scorn for Indian

A view of Cornwall, England, showing the patchwork of small fields that has characterized much of that country's landscape since the Enclosure Acts of the eighteenth and early nineteenth centuries. Though many of us tend to think that England has always looked like this, in the seventeenth and early eighteenth centuries common fields predominated, and much of the countryside was open and unfenced. The advent of commercial agriculture, which precipitated the enclosure movement, spurred emigration to the New World as well since many small or marginal farmers were forced off their land and had to seek their fortunes elsewhere.

males whose main occupation was hunting and who they viewed as lazy and idle. Most of these settlers came from a land where hunting and fishing were not serious occupations but only the pastimes of the rich and aristocratic. But what the English failed to see was that the Indian males not only hunted but also controlled and even propagated the animals that they killed through their annual burning of the underbrush in the fall, a custom which many settlers adopted though they little comprehended its significance.

Most of the English colonists thought the Indians' main purpose in burning was to clear the land and facilitate moving through the forests. Adriaen van der Donck, a Dutch settler who took a keen interest in Indian customs and traditions, came closer to the mark. He realized that the burning (which he said presented "a grand and sublime appearance") also worked "to thin out and clear the woods of all dead substances and grass, which grow better the ensuing spring." And by increasing the amount of grasses, notes William Cronon, ecological historian and author of *Changes in the Land: Indians, Colonists, and the Ecology of New England*, the Indians "not merely attracted game but helped create much larger populations of it. Indian burning promoted the increase of exactly those species whose abundance so impressed English colonists," Cronon goes on to say, "elk, deer, beaver, hare, porcupine, turkey, quail, ruffled grouse, and so on." In addition, it destroyed plant diseases and pests, including the fleas which sometimes became so noisome that the Indians had to move their villages in order to escape them.

In retrospect, it may seem obvious that a system based on so much mobility and one based on permanence would not be able to coexist. As Charles Hudson, an Indian historian, has observed, "Never in the history of the world have cultures so different and so unprepared for each other come into such ineluctable collision." Almost from the beginning, conflicts between Indians and settlers arose, taking place in the fields, forests, towns, and courts. Indian fires threatened colonial settlements, and valuable colonial livestock were often hurt in Indian hunting traps. English grazing animals did extensive damage to Indian planting fields and foraging areas. "Their cows and horses eat the grass and their hogs spoil our clam banks and we shall all be starved," Miantonomi, sachem of the Narragansett Indians, argued in 1642 in an unsuccessful attempt to incite the Montauk Indians of Long Island to join with the Narragansetts in waging war.

The frequent incursions of colonial livestock into Indian fields "provided an ironic comment," as Neal Salisbury has observed, "on the rationalizations of the English that they were the stable horticulturists while the Indians primarily roamed and hunted oblivious to notions of territoriality." Indians were quick to point out that since the colonists claimed ownership of the marauding animals (Indians claimed ownership of animals only at the point at which they were killed), they should be held responsible for the damages they did. Colonial courts did recognize the Indians' right to be compensated; however, Indians wishing compensation could not kill the offending animals, but had to capture and secure them until they were claimed by their owners——a procedure that was not always followed.

On May 15, 1631, "Chickataubott & Saggamore John" (two Massachusetts Indians who were often brought before the court of the Massachusetts Bay Colony for the revenge they and their followers took on English livestock) "pmised unto the Court to make satisfaccon for whatsoever wronge that any of their men shall doe to any of the Englishe, to their cattell or any othr waies." And on June 18 of the same year, Chickataubott was "fyned a skyn of beaur for shooteinge a swine of Sr Rich: Saltonstalls."

The court did not always rule in favor of the settlers. On November 7, 1632, it was "agreed, that Sr Richard Saltonstall shall give Saggamore John a hogshead of corne for the hurt his cattell did him in his corne." However, even in those cases where Indians were compensated, fines and punishments were always levied from the English point of view.

In different settlements, the same conflicts were repeated with much the same results. Colonists were required to give Indians "satisfaccon" for damage done to their crops, and Indians were fined (sometimes "two skins of beaver") for taking revenge on colonial cattle or for unintentional harm done by their traps. It wasn't long before the courts took the next step of requiring Indians to protect their crops. On September 4, 1632, Saggamore John "pomised against the nexte yeare, & soe euer after, to fence their corne against all kinde of cattell." In some towns, the colonists themselves began building fences to protect the Indians' corn fields. In 1653, the town of New Haven pledged sixty days of labor to construct fences on the native Quiripis' behalf. But this was on the understanding that the Indians would agree to "doe no damage to the English Cattell, and to secure their owne corne from damage or to require none"—to be, in other words, responsible for the future upkeep of their newly acquired fences.

Ultimately, Indians were forced to adopt the European method of protecting crops from livestock, the fence, even though they had no domesticated animals of their own and even though fences were fundamentally antagonistic to their way of life. It was only a matter of time before these native New Englanders, having lost their territories and their traditional means of survival, would also be erecting fences—and stone walls—for the colonists.

2

GENERATIONS OF FENCES

IN the 1600s, when the first colonists were deciding how to divide the countryside of New England and New York, how to lay down boundary lines and plan the towns around which their lives would revolve, they used as a pattern, naturally enough, the towns and villages they had left behind in the Old World. For reasons of safety (protection from Indian attacks) and familiarity, they decided that the houses with their accompanying garden plots and stables would stand close together, not far from the church, and that the fields and pasture lands would be located some distance from the town and would be held in common. Most English and Dutch settlers were used to holding land in common and to working distant fields so this system seemed logical. It was only much later, as fear of attacks subsided and settlements began to blanket New England, and as the New World's great abundance of land began to change the colonial mindset, that the system of common fields came to be seen as a waste of both time and land and farms were established as the cohesive, isolated units we know them as today.

In some parts of New England, such as the colonies of Rhode Island and Connecticut, land had originally been obtained by direct charter from the king of England. In others, it had been granted by the king to trading corporations. These corporations, the Massachusetts Bay Company, for example, then made much smaller grants of land—about six miles square on the average—to groups of settlers who wished to found a town and who, at least initially, held all the land in common. One of the first acts of any group of new townspeople was a survey to determine what different types of land——grassy areas, forest, swamp, salt marshes for cutting hay——their territory contained. Many of the early settlements were situated on abandoned Indian corn fields, sparing settlers the necessity of having to clear the ground before they could get on to the important business of planting; but later settlements were forced to begin on heavily forested land.

After a territory was surveyed, it was divided into areas for the village, home lots, tillage, pasture, and timber lands. The village was usually laid out near the center of the grant. The sites for the village green and meetinghouse were decided first, then the streets were laid out, and the land on either side of the proposed streets divided into home lots for each family. These areas would contain a family's barns, stables, and vegetable gardens; and in New England they were often assigned by lot, a method which is said to have prevented bickering and ill will because the drawing of lots represented an appeal to the judgment of God.

Each family was also assigned a portion of the common fields for tillage and mowing. The quantity of land allotted to each proprietor was the subject of serious and prayerful consideration and was determined by a rule of distribution which in many cases was agreed upon in advance. Sometimes the lots were of equal size, but often those who had a large family and, therefore, were able to use more land or those who had invested heavily in the settlement enterprise got more.

IN EARLY SETTLEMENTS, the conflicts between Indians and colonists over animals and crops mirrored those that occurred between the colonists them-selves. Stray colonial stock was, of course, also wont to destroy poorly pro-tected colonial corn. At first, the courts tried to deal with these infractions by putting English common law into practice and placing the burden of respon-sibility for animal damage on the shoulders of the animal owners. English common law doesn't actually require animal owners to enclose their stock, but it does make them legally bound to keep their livestock from trespassing and liable for any damage they do——forcing them, in effect, to keep their animals enclosed or under the watchful eye of a careful herder.

But this approach, as the colonists would come to realize, only makes sense where there is an abundance of cheap labor or at the mature stage of a settlement, when most of the arable land is under cultivation and, therefore, the cost of fencing crops is much greater than that of fencing animals. In early New England, the opposite conditions existed: there were chronic labor shortages and very little land had been cleared for planting. Fencing it would be far easier than fencing all that lay around it. This approach would also have the great advantage of allowing livestock to run free and forage food for themselves, which was, in the first, busy years in the New World, the only way that many of these animals survived.

The colonists found it difficult to break with their Old World fencing traditions, though, and for some years the courts shifted the burden of responsibility for unruly animals back and forth between the owners of crops and the owners of animals. This resulted in such ambivalent and unenforceable laws as the one passed by the court of the Massachusetts Bay Colony in 1638 which ruled that "they that plant are to secure their corne in the day time; but if the cattle do hurt corne in the night, the owners of the cattle shall make good the damages." In Plymouth in 1633, thirteen years after the landing of the *Mayflower*, the Plymouth court finally made crop growers responsible for fencing when it ordered that no one should set corn "without enclosure but at his perill." In 1642, the Massachusetts court reversed its previous ruling and declared that "every man must secure his corne and medowe against great cattell."

Thus began the body of laws and customs requiring farmers to enclose (or "restrain," as bitter planters came to say ironically) their crops, a pill that many would find increasingly bitter to swallow as land became more settled. For out of these new laws would arise many of the fencing problems of the nineteenth century. Under them, it also came to be accepted that any land not enclosed and not planted in crops was suitable pasture ground for livestock, regardless of its ownership. This land, extending to the roads and highways, was treated as common.

WITH ALL THAT needed to be done in the early settlements, the colonists' first fences were constructed as quickly as possible using whatever materials were readily at hand. Crude as many of these fences were, they signified the settlers' intention to improve the land and, therefore, their right to it. They also marked boundaries that would eventually be transcribed into stone.

In some areas, farmers first erected brush or deadwood fences, simply piling on their property lines the materials that they had cleared from the land; in others, they made wicket fences, driving stakes into the ground, then weaving in willow or other tree saplings. Where timber was especially abundant, many settlers used log fences which they constructed by stacking the trunks of trees on top of each other. Stockades, enclosures built for protection against Indian attacks, were also made in this way and were, in fact, some of the first colonial fences. In 1645, the entire town of Milford, Connecticut, was enclosed in a stockade, leading the local Indians to taunt the settlers with the phrase, "White men all same like pigs."

Livestock and Indians were not the only trespassers early settlers had to fence against. Colonial (and, probably, Indian) dogs turned out to be a substantial nuisance, especially in Plymouth where the Pilgrims were using fish as a fertilizer. To protect their gardens and crops against the dogs that would dig the fish up, the Pilgrims enclosed them with tight pale fences, a type of fence made of pointed stakes or pales driven deep into the ground and held together on top by a rail to which each pale was fastened. The predecessor of the picket fence, pale fences still enclose a few front yards on Cambridge's Tory Row.

Some of these early fences were effective while they lasted, but they did not last long. Speed rather than permanence was the most important criterion in their construction, and after a period of several years, most of these first fences needed to be replaced. In their second approach to the enduring problem of separating crops and livestock, many farmers turned to an unsightly but more effective solution: the stump fence.

Stump fences, as their name implies, were made by dragging the stumps of trees to the edge of a field and placing them side by side, with their interlacing roots facing outward and their trunks inward. In the days when "ugly as a stump fence" was a simile in common usage, the stump fence had its critics, but in 1837 one observer called it "a singular fence . . . needing no mending, and lasting the ' for ever ' of this world." "The devil himself couldn't move a stump fence," farmers used to say, an opinion borne out by the fact that stump fences well over a hundred years old can still be seen in parts of Canada and in the Midwest.

Stumps were often the product of the first clearing of the land, but stump fences didn't appear in the first generation of a settlement's fences because stumps need to sit in the ground for six to ten years before they are loose

Though this stump fence may not have been much to look at, it had considerable advantages over other types of settlement fencing. It lasted much longer and was quite an effective solution to the perennial problem of separating livestock (in this illustration, a Devon cow) and crops. The gaps in most stump fences were filled in with brush——making them even more effective barriers——so that at times it would have been difficult to tell a stump fence from a brush fence.

enough to be pulled out and hauled away. Extracting even a loosened stump was never easy; it required oxen and strong chains, something that many settlers lacked at first. In the 1800s, stump pulling would become a cash business and one way that a man could make a good living. Twenty-five cents a stump was the standard price in 1850 when men operating such mechanical stump pullers as the "Portable Goliath," "The Little Giant," and "Roger's Patent Extractor" could extract from twenty to fifty stumps a day.

An alternative to the stump fence in some areas and its predecessor in others was the zig-zag or worm fence, a portable, rail fence requiring neither posts nor holes. Worm fences were built of split rails which were laid in a zig-zag fashion with their ends interlocking at an angle of sixty degrees. Though some historians have suggested that this type of fence was a modification of an Indian hunting fence, there is no good evidence as to where or how it originated. It was used in New England before 1685, we know, because the minutes of the town of Salem, Massachusetts, record the construction of a "new worme fence about the meeting house at Alloway's Creek."

Despite its obscure origins, by 1871, the year of the Department of Agriculture's fencing survey, sixty percent of all the fencing in the United States was zig-zag. Its ubiquitousness was reflected in the number of states it was used in—all thirty nine—and the number of names it was known by, which included Virginia rail fence, rail fence, crooked rail fence, worm fence, zig-zag fence, snake fence, jig-jag fence, rick-rack fence, and lazyman's fence.

Of all the different kinds of fencing used by early settlers, the worm fence illustrates best that the key factor driving the choice of fencing in new settlements was the relationship between labor and lumber. The worm fence required a maximum of lumber—which many of the colonists had—and a minimum of time and labor—which they did not. A man handy with an ax and a wedge could cut 150 to 200 ten-foot rails in a day; at the same time, his co-worker could convert those rails into 200 yards of fence. (Given the same amount of time, two wall builders might have laid only ten feet of stone wall.) So even though zig-zag fencing took up a great deal of land that could otherwise be cultivated (five acres of land for every square mile of land fenced) and rotted very rapidly (especially when made of oak rather than the preferred woods, chestnut and cedar), it caught on rapidly. More labor-intensive fencing—post and rail fences, board fences, and stone walls—was not usually undertaken until a farmer either found himself with time on his hands or a shortage of trees.

There were, of course, some exceptions. Some farmers may have turned to building stone walls earlier than others because of a natural bent for wall building or because, being well endowed with sons, they went through the laborious stages of clearing more quickly than others. Also, in many pockets of New England and New York—Connecticut's Hampton area and eastern Rhode Island, for example—local rock formations resulted in an abundance of easily split sheets and slabs of schists, quartzites, and sandstones that made wall building easy. In those areas, stone walls, or stone fences as they were also known, were sometimes found as early as the 1640s and 1650s. In Bedford, New York, there is some good building stone, and the records of 1687 from that town make note that "3 foots and a half high" was considered to be an adequate "stone fence" whereas a "good logg fence" was "foure foot and halfe high" and "a good raile fence" was "four foot high at least."

The construction of most of New England's stone walls, however, had to wait until the near total deforestation of the area. These walls were, in fact, due as much to that deforestation as they were to the glaciers that deposited the stone on the land in the first place. Had the colonists not been so profligate with wood, these walls might never have been built.

It must have been impossible for the earliest settlers of New England and New York to imagine the rapidity with which their land—through the combined activities of clearing, commercial lumbering, construction, and fuel consumption—would be transformed from forest to treeless land. In 1656, Adriaen van der Donck wrote that "there actually is such an abundance of wood in the New Netherlands, that, with ordinary care, it will never be scarce there."

Van der Donck was a good observer but not very prophetic. For when the colonists, many of whom came from regions of the Netherlands and England that were practically destitute of timber, were confronted by this abundance, they quickly abandoned many of their Old World, conservationist habits: half

Worm, zig-zag, or Virginia rail
fencing required a maximum of
timber, but a minimum of time and
was quickly adopted in all of the
colonies. In the 1800s, when 60
percent of the fencing in the
United States was of this type, a
dishonest man was said to be "as
crooked as a rail fence."

timber-half stone construction, thatched and slate roofs, and infrequent hearth fires. The trees of New England came to mean to the colonists "being warm in winter, warmer than even the nobility of England could hope to be," and between 1630 and 1800, it is estimated that New Englanders consumed more than 260 million cords of firewood. According to William Cronon, a typical household consumed as much as thirty to forty cords of firewood a year which, he suggests, is best visualized as a stack of wood four feet high, four feet wide and three hundred feet long. Towns often experienced shortages of wood within a decade of their settlement, and certain individuals wondered if the "increasing evil" of deforestation would "put a final stop to the progress of population."

Some historians have argued that early measures were taken to preserve the timber resources of the colonies, but others disagree, noting that the colonists consistently violated conservation laws and "used forests as if they would last forever."

As Perr Kalm, a Finnish botanist and traveler in the American colonies in the 1740s, observed, "if one considers that worm fences are crooked and require a greater quantity of material than if they were straight, that they must be replaced in a comparatively short time, and if one considers also the unbelievable quantity of wood burned day and night in every room in the house throughout the winter, one sees what punishment the forest is taking and wonders how it will look in thirty or fifty years."

Kalm couldn't have been more accurate, even in his timing. Many areas suffered wood shortages as early as the seventeenth century, but shortages became widespread and acute after the Revolutionary War. Fencing was particularly affected, since in the course of the war many fences had been burned either for fuel or in battle. When it came time to rebuild them, farmers found themselves without any trees. In rocky areas, farmers began to build a new generation of fences out of stone, using in most cases, the stones that men before them had cleared from the land and left in piles, usually along the boundary lines. (Interestingly, this transition from wood to stone took place in fencing but not in housing. Though building stone is plentiful in New England, the early abundance of timber and the cost and difficulties of quarrying, transporting, and handling stone determined the form that colonial architecture took—a type of wooden building little used in Europe—and later shortages were never so great as to cause most New Englanders to abandon it. The Dutch settlers of New York were the most likely to replace their first wooden dwellings with ones made of brick or stone.)

In New England these new fences went by a number of different names, though stone wall was by far the most common and was used in every New England state, as well as in New York. In Maine they were also known as rock walls and rock fences, and in Cape Cod and parts of Connecticut, stone fences, a name common in Pennsylvania and western New York as well. In northern New Jersey, the only part of New Jersey with a good supply of surface stone, they were called stone rows. Many New Englanders used fence and wall interchangeably, though some reserved the term "stone fence" for a wall that was part stone and part wood, and others, for a wall that was carefully laid, as

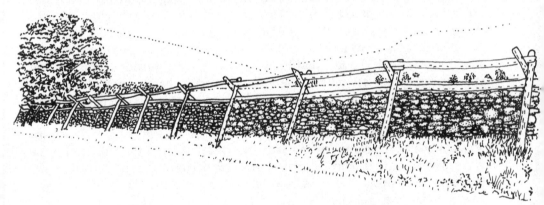

In parts of New England and New York where stone was scarce, walls were topped with rails, brush, or, as in this case, stakes and riders to give them additional height. "In Middlesex [Connecticut] where a poor quality of stone is available," reported the Department of Agriculture's 1871 fencing survey, "walls 3 feet high are common, with stakes and rails above. In New Haven similar fences are made, the wall 2 1/2 feet high."

opposed to a hastily built one. In areas where stone was particularly abundant, such as southern New Hampshire, these new fences could be five feet high or up to eight feet wide. In areas where it was scarce, they were often low—just two to three feet high—and topped with rails, riders, or even brush, to give them additional height.

For more than a hundred years, the soil of glacial New England had frustrated efforts at cultivation, but farmers were now looking at their rocky heritage in a slightly new light. Wooden fences came to be regarded, as Thomas Jefferson once put it, as a "great and perishable work" and stone ones were suddenly the fences of choice and common sense. Accounts of New England described those areas that were lacking in stone for fencing as being seriously disadvantaged, and farmers' dictionaries began to advise their readers to build their fences of stone.

"When the ground is wholly fubdued, and the ftumps of its original growth of trees quite rotted out," notes the *New England Farmer or Georgical Dictionary* of 1790, "if ftones can be had without carrying too far, ftone walls are the fences that ought to be made. Though the coft may be greater at firft than that of fome other fences, they will prove to be cheapeft in the end."

The fact that farmers heeded this advice had as much to do with its soundness as with the fact that by the end of the eighteenth century, many farmers had the tools to build stone walls: crow bars, chains, a pair of oxen, and a stone boat (a flat runnerless sled used for hauling stone), as well as the time. By then, the land in at least the early settlements of southern New England was well cleared (in later settlements in New Hampshire, Vermont, and western Massachusetts, the same fencing sequence of brush, stumps, rails, and stone walls was repeated), and farmers could now spare the time for this labor-intensive task. Most of them had no alternative; either they built walls or their cows got into their neighbor's corn.

Stone-wall building began in earnest, and most of the predecessors of these walls—the earlier fences of brush and rails—disappeared without a trace. One of the most curious of New England fences, the zig-zag stone wall, however, accurately preserves the form of its wooden ancestor. Why would anyone build a zig-zag fence out of stone? Nobody would set out to do such a thing deliberately. But a farmer would have put up a worm fence around his field and would have tossed stones against that fence as he cleared them out of his land. Before long, the original wooden fence would rot and he or his son, or perhaps his grandson, would be left with a chimera of a fence, a pile of rocks with the backbone of a zig-zag fence but with flesh of stone.

3

As American as . . . a Fence Viewer or a Town Pound

AFTER the courts of New England ruled that planters were responsible for fencing their crops, the fencing problems of the colonies did not, of course, come to an end. The hastily constructed fencing put up in the early days of a settlement was not always effective—large, obstreperous (or just hungry) animals could often get to the other side of any fence they set their minds on, and conflicts were inevitable. Many settlers nearly came to blows over questions of whose fences were adequate, whose animals unruly.

In order to handle these conflicts, New England towns created the office of fence viewer, an appointed official who regularly made the rounds of a town's fences to "see that the fence be sett in good repair, or else complain of it." Fence viewers noted breaks in fences and ordered repairs. If a fence was declared sound by the viewer, its owner would be able to collect damages should an animal break through it. If a fence was declared unsound, the owner was unprotected by law and was usually required to repair the fence within a certain amount of time or to pay double recompense to those who did repair it—often the fence viewer. The fence viewers, in turn, were liable (by fine) for the neglect of fences within their jurisdiction, a seemingly excellent but curiously out-of-favor method of ensuring that someone was actually going to do

Long walks on cold days would keep a New England fence viewer wrapped up in his frock coat and plug hat. This town official has just crossed what is probably a cow stile (a stile designed to let people, but not cows, pass from one field to another) on his way, perhaps, to settling another thorny dispute.

the job for which he was being paid. As of 1642, the Colonial Laws of Massachusetts ordered that

> the Select men of every town shall appoint, from year to year, two or more ... to view the Common fences, of all their Corn-fields, to the end, to take notice of the real defects and insufficiency thereof, who shall forthwith acquaint the owners thereof with the same; and if the said Owners do not within six dayes time or otherwise as the Select men shall appoint, sufficiently repair their said defective fences: then the said two or more Inhabitants appointed as aforesaid, shall forthwith repair or reniew them, and shall have double recompence for all their labour, care, cost, and trouble, to be paid by the Owners of the said insufficient Fence or Fences, and shall have warrant from the said Select men, directed to the Constable to levy the same, either upon the Corn or other estate of the Delinquent: Provided the defect of the Fence or Fences be sufficiently proved by two or three witnesses.

At first, the fences that the viewers were concerned with were the communal fences surrounding the "great lotts" or common tillage fields. These were erected and kept in repair by those who held shares in the fields, with each man being responsible for a length of fence proportionate to his allotment and required to work on his section for a certain amount of time each year or to pay his share for the work of others. As generations passed, though, and more and more of a town's common lands came to be divided up and assigned to individuals, the fence viewer came to be responsible for private as well as communal fences. These fences might still surround tillage fields or they might be the fences defining a farmer's property line.

Fence viewers were responsible for making sure that these fences were sound and that they were of the height required by a town. In the beginning, the settlers of Guilford, Connecticut, were ordered to set their fences at four feet; by 1653, a "sufficient fence" had to be four and a half feet high. By the late 1670s, many towns were insisting on fences five feet high and on stone walls of four feet, though some areas still had less exacting requirements. In 1710, the

Laws of the Royal Colony of New Jersey stated "that all Fences that are and shall be made hereafter, and esteemed to be good, lawful and sufficient against Cattle and Horses, shall be Four Foot and Four Inches High." In Vermont today, a legal fence must be at least four and a half feet high, a requirement that dates back to 1780, and of such construction that sheep cannot get over it. Sometimes specifications were more humorous than precise. In 1868, a Vermont newspaper published an anecdote about three fence viewers, one of whom was heavy, one short, and one tall. A fence was deemed adequate when the heavy one could sit on it without breaking it, the short one couldn't get under it, and the tall one couldn't straddle it.

In some towns, viewers were also required to walk the boundaries of the town once a year, usually in the company of the town selectmen—an annual ritual also known, as it was in England where the tradition came from, as "perambulating the bounds" or "beating the bounds." The ritual was performed in order to determine if any neighboring towns were encroaching on a town's land. To make certain that this did not happen, some towns went to the pain of erecting stone walls along their boundary lines. In early Connecticut, the boundary line between the towns of Norwalk and Stamford—established in 1686—was a stone wall called the Perambulation Line. As you traveled north from the coast, all the land on the right-hand side of the wall lay in Norwalk; on the left, in Stamford. No landowner in the area need ever have been in doubt as to where he should file his deeds and pay his taxes. When the town of New Canaan—situated between Norwalk and Stamford—became incorporated in 1801, the Perambulation Line ceased to have any meaning and much of the wall was dismantled. Bits and pieces still remain, and according to New Canaan historian Mary Louise King, one short stretch runs behind the house lots on the west side of Kimberly Place; another angles through the wood just east of Lapham High School's lower parking lot.

As more and more of New England was cleared and fenced, the office of fence viewer grew in importance. Fence viewers usually wore the uniform of a town official—a plug hat and frock coat—and in wealthier towns, they may have had several assistants or deputies, two of whom would have been responsible for doing the measuring of acreage and fence lengths using what was once a very familiar device——a Gunter's chain. A Gunter's chain is a sixty-six-foot long chain made up of one hundred links; it was invented in 1620 by Edmund Gunter, an English preacher turned mathematician who is also known for his invention of the sector and for introducing the words cosine and

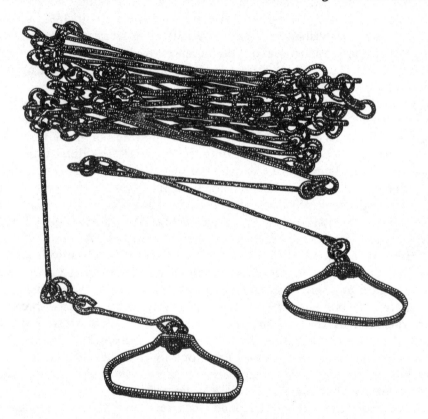

A precursor of the modern measuring tape, the sixty-six-foot long Gunter's chain could not have been light to carry or easy to use in the cold winter months. It was made of malleable iron and consisted of one hundred links with a handle at either end.

cotangent into the English vocabulary. The great usefulness of a Gunter's chain in surveying comes from its division into one hundred parts and from the fact that ten square chains equal an acre (66 feet x 66 feet x 10 = 43,560 square feet) and eighty chain lengths equal a mile (80 x 66 feet = 5,280 feet). The chain is the reason behind many of the measurements used until recent times. City blocks, for instance, were laid out to equal three chains, and telegraph poles were placed either one or two chains apart. The width of a city street, or that of a canal, was set at one chain.

Distances shorter than a chain were measured in rods and links. A rod, known sometimes as a "pole" or a "perch," is sixteen and a half feet long or one-fourth of a chain, so rods were also called "quarter-chains." All of these measurements appear again and again in the decisions and renderings of colonial and postcolonial fence viewers, decisions that were always filed with the town. One of these renderings, a decision made in 1834 by two fence viewers in Wenham, Massachusetts, is typical in both its content and the breathless style in which it was written.

Whereas a dispute has arisen between Jacob Dodge and Elizabeth Street of Wenham about the respective rights in a partition fence in the line between their lands on farms in Wenham, we the subscribers [sic] fence viewers of Wenham duly chosen and sworn having on the application of the said Jacob Dodge after having given due notice to the said Elizabeth Street viewed the premises and duly considered the matter in disput have assign'd and do hereby assign to each of said parties his share of said fence as follows.

The said Jacob Dodge shall build and keep in repair a good and sufficient fence from Paul Porters wall running northerly seven rods and fourteen links to an apple tree stump standing in the said fence. & the said Elizabeth Street shall build and keep in repair the fence from the last named bounds running northerly twenty rods to the southwesterly corner of the barn. The said Jacob Dodge shall build and maintain a fence commencing at a stake in the wall on the East side of the barn near an apple tree and running northerly forty-eight rods to the stake and stones on the side of the wall then the said Elizabeth Street shall build and maintain the fence commencing at the last named bounds and running northerly to the corner of Elizabeth Streets third thirty five rods and we do hereby assign the term of thirty days for making up said fence wereof the several parties aforesaid are to take notice given under our hands and seals this 22 day of April 1834.

    William Moulton } Fence Viewers for Wenham
    Nicholas Dodge }

These "agreements to build fence," as they were called, make interesting reading not just because they point out the importance of fencing in agricultural New England. (It was, after all, all that stood between a settlement and starvation. In 1659, the punishment for "stripping fences of rails and posts" in the New Netherlands was a whipping and branding for a first offence and death for a second, a punishment which may have been unusually harsh but was certainly understandable given that in 1659, the New Netherlands was experiencing a serious shortage of grain and other foodstuffs.) They also chart the use and changes in fencing materials. As we have seen, fences made of stone were usually late additions to the colonial landscape, which is very much reflected in the fencing agreements of many towns. In early agreements from a town, stone walls are mentioned rarely, if at all. In later ones, they may be the fence type most frequently referred to.

Over the last 150 years, as agriculture has become a smaller part of New England's economic picture, fencing and the office of fence viewer have, of course, declined in importance. But with all the changes that have taken place, fencing—though it has altered much in function and appearance—has not disappeared from the landscape and neither has this New England official. Many towns still have statutes on their books that require appointing one or more fence viewers, and though most of today's appointees look upon this as something of a joke, some take their jobs very seriously. The issues they are called in to settle may be more emotional than economic, but they still require careful handling.

Listen, for example, to Richard Lasher, who has been a fence viewer in Wethersfield, Connecticut, for more than twelve years. "In today's disputes over fences, the fences are usually symbols," says Lasher. "The people are really mad about something else but they focus on the fence. The fence might have been there fifteen years, then all of a sudden..."

Wethersfield is a residential suburb of Hartford and if its fences serve to keep any animals in or out today, they are only dogs. Not too long ago, though, Wethersfield was dairy country and before that it was populated by the same self-sufficient farmers who farmed most of New England. The town had its first fence viewer in 1645, Robert Francis, who is best remembered for his testimony at a witchcraft trial when a Wethersfield woman was charged with causing the explosion of a barrel of cider and killing a sick child.

Many things have changed about the job of fence viewer since Francis's time, but the qualities needed to be a good fence viewer have stayed the same. Lasher, the modern fence viewer, says that he has to be part psychologist and know how to work with people and enjoy doing it. Wethersfield's statutes state that he should be paid $2 a day, but Lasher insists that he has never accepted anything for the twenty-two disputes that he has been called in on.

THE OFFICE OF FENCE viewer was not the only American invention to arise out of the conflicting needs of crops and animals (and the way New Englanders chose to handle them). The other was the town pound: a simple, roofless corral or enclosure where animals found straying into fields or gardens could be brought and held until they were collected by their owners and fines paid.

In England, most livestock had been watched over by individual herders, but in New England, labor was so scarce that only the most valuable animals—milk cows, sheep, and some horses and oxen—were guarded in this way. The rest—swine, goats, and dry cattle—were left to their own devices, thereby posing a constant threat to crops. Efforts were made to graze stock in areas far removed from settlements, but inevitably some animals wandered back from these distant forests or isolated peninsulas and managed to do substantial damage. By 1635, the court of Massachusetts had ordered the towns under its jurisdiction to construct pounds to which swine could be taken whenever they were found within one mile of an English farm. The swine, like other animals, were identified by marks on their ears——slits, crops, and ha'pennies on one ear or both——which were registered with the town. Crops were cuts across the tip of the ear; ha'pennies, half circles cut on the edge; and slits, longitudinal cuts that divided the ear into two parts.

Like most town pounds dating from the early nineteenth century, the pounds of Auburn and Chester, New Hampshire, are rectangular with walls about four feet wide and six feet high. Auburn's pound was built in 1843 and takes advantage of a natural rock ledge for one of its walls. The Chester pound was constructed in 1804 and utilizes an especially beautiful and large, uncut stone for its lintel. Both pounds became obsolete sometime in the nineteenth century and have since been used more by wild animals, such as the gray fox pictured here, than domesticated ones.

One of the earliest recorded pounds was built in the town of Scituate, Massachusetts, in 1634, but it must have been built of wood for it did not survive long. A second pound built in 1781 on the same site and of stone stands today. Sometimes the barnyard of a specific farmer served the town as a

pound; othertimes, pounds were specially erected after a town made such a recommendation. Many of these pounds were commissioned with the requirement that they be built "horse high, bull strong and hog tight," but some had more detailed and precise specifications. On March 3, 1806, the town of Whitingham, Vermont, "voted to build a pound of stone in the following dimensions: 30 feet squair within the walls, the walls to be six feet high four feet thick at the bottom two feet thick on the top frame together with a Stone Post to Hang the Door or gate on with a hole drilled in the Said Post for the Hinges to be set in, Said Pound to be completed by the first Day of July next, Said Walls to be Handsomely faced on the inside and Decently faced on the outside to the acceptance of the Select Men." The bill for this imposing edifice came to $34.98.

Though a town's prosperity had a direct bearing on the size and quality of its pound, most New Englanders learned quickly that it paid to build their pounds well. The stone pounds that are still standing today (and stone pounds are the only pounds to have survived to this day) provide some of the finest examples of wall building in New England. Like the one in Whitingham, Vermont, many of these pounds are square enclosures with walls about thirty feet on a side and about six feet tall; but some pounds are rectangular, circular, or even trapezoidal. Among the surviving pounds, some are extremely impressive—for their height (one in Richmond, Rhode Island, is over eight feet tall), their width (many are four feet thick), the enormous size of the stones used in their construction, and their idiosyncratic design features. A pound in Forster Center, Rhode Island, for example, was built around two brooks. The animals in that pound may have had muddy feet, but they never needed watering.

For what may be obvious reasons, few aspired to the office of pound-keeper. On call, the poundkeeper had to run down stray pigs, catch wandering horses, confront bulls, and wrestle loose rams. He also had to pay out of his own pocket the expenses of feeding animals, sometimes with little hope of ever being able to collect from the owner. Because of the unpopularity of the position, some towns resorted to forcing the job upon the man who had most recently married as of that year's town meeting. In other towns, the post was only filled by making it the first apprenticeship of would-be politicians. One only wishes for as good a way of testing those who would run for office today.

Though the traditions of fence viewers and town pounds arose at about the same time and out of the same set of circumstances, one didn't last nearly as long as the other. The town pound didn't even last as long as agriculture dominated New England. Pounds were necessary only as long as most of New England's animals were pastured on common, unfenced lands. As towns divided up their common lands and farmers began to enclose their stock individually, town pounds became relics of the past. By the late 1800s, most of them had fallen into disuse, surviving only in the very modified form of today's dog pounds.

PART II

SERMONS IN STONES

4

SERMONS IN STONES

EVERY spring when the farmers of New England spiked their fields clear of stones and boulders, they had to wonder. Where had all these stones come from? Hadn't they picked the fields clean just last year? Wasn't the ground as smooth as butter when they plowed it last in the fall? Few of them could have understood the reason behind this spring crop of rock——that the freezing and thawing of groundwater works to heave up rocks from deep in the earth and that plowing itself accelerates this process——and some began to see the mysterious reappearance of stones in previously cleared fields as the work of the devil. It was he who placed them there to try to break their faith——and backs.

Others came to swear that stones grew in the soil from seed—like potatoes. "Maine's number-two crop is potatoes," runs a saying still in use today. "Its number-one crop is stones." "When you buy meat, you buy bones," begins another New England maxim. "When you buy land, you buy stones."

Ezra Stiles, president of Yale University in the eighteenth century, used to enjoy reciting a rhyme his father had written about the family farm in Cornwall, Connecticut. "Nature out of her boundless store / Threw rocks together, and did no more."

At least one farmer's experience with the stones in his fields left him unable to accept that the earth turns on its axis. For if the earth did "go round" and his farm ever "got bottom side up," that farmer insisted, "there would be a great rattling of stones below," and he would be saved the trouble of getting any more stones off his land.

"It is quite true that there are sermons in stones," F. Ratchford Starr, a farmer from Litchfield, Connecticut, once wrote. "The earth too is a sermonizer of no mean order."

BUT NEW ENGLAND did not always preach such a sermon in stones. Before the glaciers of the Pleistocene Ice Age, long before there were any farmers to turn the ground and puzzle over its mysteries, New England was covered, not with rocks, but with thick residual soils, soils much like those in the Carolinas. Before the Ice Age, New England, which is geologically a very ancient part of the world, had also been a landscape of valleys and divides with many rivers and streams but few if any lakes. Its mountains, which were formed some 350 million years ago, once rivaled the Himalayas.

About two and a half million years ago, the first of the four glaciers of the Pleistocene era began moving down from the north, covering New England with a sheet of ice that may have been in many places almost a mile thick, as thick as three World Trade Centers, stacked one on top of another, thicker by over a thousand feet than the George Washington Bridge upended. When the last glacier—the Wisconsin—retreated just 12,000 to 14,000 years ago, it left behind a warmer climate and a transformed landscape, a landscape scrawled with the glaciers' signature.

The glaciers had accomplished their dramatic transformation of the landscape through erosion and deposition. During the many millions of years between the time when New England's mountains had been formed and the onset of the Ice Age, those mountains had weathered enormously and were covered with what geologists refer to as "rotten" or soft rock. As the glaciers moved over this rotten rock, it was incorporated into the underside of the ice sheets by a process known as "glacial quarrying" or "plucking." Four glaciers later, the ancient mountains were scraped clean, leaving behind the worndown stumps which we now know as the Green Mountains of Vermont and

A scale drawing of the Hartford skyline set against a fictitious glacier, also drawn to scale. Like the glaciers of the Pleistocene era, this one is almost a mile thick.

the White Mountains of New Hampshire. Their rocks had been strewn over the New England countryside and refashioned into Long Island. The thick residual soils that had once covered New England had also been scoured away, leaving the area with much bare rock but also some fertile regions where the glaciers dumped these same materials.

Geologists tell us to look at the glacier as a conveyor belt that stopped at Long Island, its terminal moraine or endpoint where much of the material it carried was finally dumped. Like a conveyer belt, it only carried material in one direction, but a lot of things fell out along the way, including acres of fine-grained materials—clays and silts—and tons of rocks.

Geologists call these rocks glacial erratics: erratics because they are not

This knob of granite has been sculpted by the glaciers. As ice sheets moved south (in the direction that the Mallard ducks are facing), they grooved, polished, and rounded the underlying bedrock, using as their tools the rocks, large and small, which were dragged along with them. On the southern face of this knob, large pieces of rock have also been plucked away in the process known as glacial quarrying.

indigenous to the place of their occurrence and glacial erratics because they were transported from a more northerly position by the glacial ice. They range in size from a marble to a henhouse or a small garage. Glacial quarrying is the name for the process by which the glaciers picked up these rocks and transported them south. One might imagine that a glacier acts like a snowball as it is rolled, picking up leaves, grass, and small pebbles, but what really happens is far more interesting.

The ice on the underside of a glacier—the basal ice that comes in contact with soil and rocks—is in a constant state of fluctuation between freezing and thawing, solid and liquid, ice and water. This basal ice has hundreds of feet of ice above it, pressing down upon it, and thereby lowering its melting point. As water, it flows around and envelopes a rock over which the glacier is passing. But when that water freezes into ice, the rock is pulled loose with a tremendous force. This process allows loose debris—silt, sand, and small stones—to be incorporated into a moving ice mass. Also incorporated are very large pieces of rock, especially rock that is well-jointed, such as rock with many fracture planes or cracks. Once incorporated into the glacier, these rocks become the abrasive tools that scratch, polish, and groove the landscape as the glacier moves south.

WHEN THE FIRST colonists arrived in the New World from the Netherlands and England, they found the glacial erratics much as the glaciers had left them. Though Indian tribes had been farming the area for almost a thousand years, their choice of crops and crop land (the stoneless flood plains) and their agricultural techniques did not necessitate clearing the stones from the land. To prepare an area for planting corn and squash, New England's original farmers simply destroyed the trees and underbrush, then worked around roots and any rocks with clam shell hoes and mattocks. The result was an agriculture that looked messy and haphazard to the colonists though they had to admire its productivity. "They know nothing of ploughing spading and spitting up the soil and are not neat and cleanly in their fields," van der Donck remarked of the Indians in the New Netherlands. Though "they take very little care" of

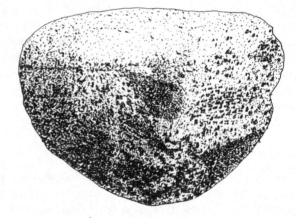

Often, something of the history of New England's field stones can be told just by their shape. Very round stones, known as cobbles, are stones that were tumbled in one of the fast-moving streams created during the melting of a glacier. Stones that are only somewhat rounded may have been transported in the ice sheets themselves; while those that are extremely angular are the natural result of the weathering of rock outcrops.

their fields, "they raise an abundance of corn and beans, of which we obtain whole cargos in sloops and galleys in trade."

By contrast, the colonists did not believe a crop could be raised on new land until it had been cleared of trees and stones and then "stubbed," the roots of all trees and shrubs dug out. At first, a dearth of plows and oxen forced settlers to resort to the Indians' methods and crops, but as soon as tools and animals were available the colonists began preparing the ground as they thought it ought to be prepared and for the crops—wheat and vegetables— they desired. This was an arduous task, the demands of which, as some historians have observed, helped to create the Protestant work ethic. In a single year, a settler could only hope to clear an acre or two; it took about a half a century—a lifetime of work—to carve out a farm of one hundred acres. Though the settlers did not know it, through their thorough clearing of the land they were also preparing the way for increased weed growth, soil erosion, moisture loss, and that annual spring crop of rocks that so tried their faith—agricultural side effects that Indian clearing methods had always kept to a minimum.

Working individually or communally, settlers began clearing a piece of land by either girdling or chopping down the trees. Girdling was an Indian technique borrowed by many settlers because it made far quicker work of a forest than did an ax, though it also posed considerable risks. To girdle a tree, one stripped the bark away from a section of it, thereby killing it. It was then possible to work among the leafless skeletons; however, one always had to be on guard against falling trunks.

After the trees were either chopped down or girdled, the settlers set to digging out the stones and the roots. Sometimes these tasks were mixed with pleasure, as Samuel Griswold Goodrich, a noted nineteenth-century author of juvenilia, observed in his autobiography. "We used to have 'stone bees,'" Goodrich wrote in 1856, "when all the men of a village or hamlet came together with their draft of cattle and united to clear some patch of earth which had been stigmatized by nature with an undue visitation of stones and rocks. All this labor was gratuitously rendered, save only that the proprietor of the land furnished the grog. Such a meeting was always of course a very social and sociable affair. When the work was done, gymnastic exercises——such as hopping, wrestling, and foot-racing——took place among the athletic young men."

The colonists called the stones that they found littering their fields "field stones" or sometimes "hardheads" or "cobbles," and their account books and daily journals are filled with mentions of how they toiled, sweated, and broke countless fingers as they picked, hauled, and blasted the rocks out of the soil, leaving them in piles along their boundary lines. Later generations used oxen, chains, stone boats, and crowbars to make them into walls, but even with all the right tools building walls out of field stones was never easy.

Because they were glacier tumbled, field stones were somewhat rounded and, therefore, very difficult to lay in a wall. They did have one big advantage, though, for at the same time that these stones were being glacier tumbled, they were also being glacier tested. The only stones that survived a trip in a glacier were stones that were extremely hard, such as stones made of granite and gneiss. This hardness meant that they were difficult to split, but once they were properly placed in a wall, they were also resistant to all kinds of weathering. Walls made of field stones were walls that tended to stand up well. By contrast, farmers who built their walls out of some of the indigenous materials in their area——in Westchester, New York, Westchester schist, for example——had to repair those walls after just a few seasons as some of the rocks were susceptible to weathering and flaking.

Not all areas of New England were equally rocky. Some, like parts of Maine, were so boulder strewn that many prospective farmers soon turned to other occupations——fishing, lumbering, and fruit growing——to eke out a living. Others, like the Connecticut Valley, had an abundance of rich soil and few rocks. Rhode Island's Narragansett country had an abundance of both rich soil and good building stone. Some areas, such as Long Island, were covered with cobblestones, stones so well-rounded that they looked as though they had been "washed for a long time by a mass of superincumbent water," as one colonist observed.

Most took these rounded stones as proof that the land upon which they were found had once been covered with water and, therefore, as evidence of the biblical flood. Indeed, the Deluge does account very neatly for the quantity of rounded stones found by early New Englanders, as well as for some of their other finds such as the many marine fossils that farmers in inland parts of New Jersey, New York, and Pennsylvania discovered. Those fossils actually dated from a period 400 million years earlier when there was a large salt-water basin in an area that included parts of those three states. As the Appalachian Mountain chain formed during the Paleozoic period, the sediments of this basin were pushed up and hardened into fossil-laden outcrops of limestones, shales, and sandstones. Farmers observed the clamlike and fishlike forms in the rocks that they cleared from their fields and made into walls (in which the fossils can be clearly seen today), but they took such oddities as more evidence of the Deluge.

Also remarked upon by the early colonists, but not so readily accounted for by the biblical Deluvian theory——the theory that dominated geological thinking until well into the 1800s——were the very large glacial erratics of New England and New York. These were usually described as "curiosities." One in Durham, New Hampshire, which Dr. James Mease said appeared to "be natural," in his 1807, *A Geological Account of the United States,* was computed to weigh sixty to seventy tons and described by Mease as lying "so exactly poised on another rock, as to be easily moved with one finger." Daniel Delavan, an eighteenth-century resident of North Salem, New York, wrote of a perched erratic measuring "fifty five feet five inches by forty three feet nine inches" that was "much noticed by travellers and affords matter of speculation for the curious how it should come in that situation whether by nature or art." As we shall see, this particular rock, which stands today just off Route 121, is still affording much "matter of speculation."

Elsewhere, in Europe, glacial erratics very much like the ones that the early farmers of New England were finding in their fields, products of the same period of glaciation, were also being noticed and commented on. There, they were beginning to prick a hole in the Deluge theory. These glacial erratics, the stuff of the walls of New England and northern Europe, were forcing people to look for alternative explanations for the geological phenomena around them and to open their eyes to the possibility of a previous period of widespread glaciation.

In 1779, the Swiss physicist and Alpine traveler Horace Benedict de Saussure introduced the whole issue when he described huge boulders of granite resting on the limestone of the Jura Mountains in Switzerland. He was the first to call these boulders "erratics," but he contended that they had been swept to their present position by torrents of water——even though their nearest possible source lay in croppings of granite sixty miles away. Some began to dispute his conclusions and assert instead that these large erratics were evidence of an ancient glaciation; but for a long time, theirs was the minority opinion. Most geologists thought the idea that large rocks were dragged over the ground by ice sheets, scratching deep marks as they went, was absurd.

Charles Lyell, a Scottish scientist of independent means, attempted to strike a compromise between the advocates of flood and those of ice by suggesting that the erratics had been transported by icebergs and ice rafts during the flood. As geologists began to perform serious studies of existing icebergs, though, evidence in favor of glaciation grew. In Switzerland, Johann von Charpentier observed that glaciers do indeed move slowly and that embedded pebbles and stones in their underside scrape and gouge the rocks over which they pass. His work attracted the attention of Louis Agassiz, a paleontologist who had been born and raised in the Swiss Alps and had made his reputation studying fossil fish. In 1837, Agassiz astounded European scientists by proposing that Europe and Asia had once been covered with glaciers that had extended as far south as the shores of the Mediterranean and Caspian seas.

The reception to Agassiz's theory was frosty, and he was told that he would do well to return to his fossil fishes. He returned instead to the Alps where he built a hut on the Aar glacier in order to better study the structure and movement of existing ice sheets. Agassiz took skeptical colleagues on athletic tours of areas of the Jura mountains and showed them rocks——many miles from any existing ice——which had been polished smooth by the passage of former ice sheets. In 1840 he published his landmark *Etude sur les glaciers*, and in the same year he took his theory to Scotland and England where he found more and more evidence of former glaciation—although not a significantly better reception. In 1846, he came to North America to travel and lecture, but was so taken by both the professional opportunities offered him and the geology of North America—a geology which showed everywhere signs of the same recent glaciation—that he decided to stay.

At first, Americans were as reluctant to accept Agassiz's glacier theory as the Europeans had been. In the 1850s Benjamin Silliman, a prominent professor of chemistry at Yale University, was still resisting the idea that glaciers could have occurred on this continent. He argued that North America does not have mountains high enough to support perennial snow. Dictionaries from the same period continued to describe glaciers as interesting phenomena that were restricted to Switzerland and that ranged in length from a mere 10 to 15 miles

and in height from 300 to 600 feet. During the 1860s, though, studies of Greenland made available much information on existing glaciers, and Agassiz's views were slowly and widely absorbed. It helped, perhaps, that he was a brilliant and popular speaker who liked to describe his adventures and communicate his love of nature to lecture-hall audiences up and down the East Coast.

When Agassiz died in 1873 he was buried at the Mount Auburn Cemetery in Cambridge, Massachusetts; his tombstone was an erratic taken from the moraine of the glacier of the Aar, not far from the site where his hut had once stood. It was a fitting monument to the man who had rewritten recent geological history to include that not too long ago, one-third of the earth had been covered with ice.

New England's early settlers had also used field stones as burial markers. They had recognized their durability and hardness (field stones are so hard that it was a job even to scratch the initials of the deceased in them), but they had not known what tales those rocks had to tell about colder times. Even if they had, it wouldn't have altered the labor involved in removing those stones from the ground and arranging them into walls. One man's glacial erratic will always be another man's field stone.

5

ERRATIC THOUGHTS

TODAY when the facts of the Ice Age have been largely accepted by all but a fundamentalist few, most people look upon glacial erratics and the stone walls they engendered as modern-day mementos of more frigid times. But there are also people who have a wholly different scenario for how certain stone walls and glacial phenomena—large rocks that are perched on a set of smaller stones, for instance—came to be. Louis Agassiz may not have been aware of it, but these ideas were emerging at about the same time that his Ice Age theory was gaining widespread acceptance. Since that time, they have continued to simmer away on a kind of ideological back burner, bubbling up into periods of intense interest, usually when a new theory or book is presented to the public.

These alternative theories were inspired—as was glaciation theory—in part by glacial erratics. One glacial erratic in particular, the large perched stone in North Salem, New York, seems to have been the most responsible. The residents of North Salem had puzzled over this stone for generations, and it was well known as a local curiosity. John Jay II, the grandson of the first chief justice of the United States and a denizen of nearby Katonah, New York, was certainly familiar with it. In 1869, Jay, an ardent abolitionist and prominent jurist in his own right (as a young man, in the years before the abolition movement was popular, even in the northern states, Jay had attained considerable notoriety for defending fugitive slaves in the New York courts), was appointed minister to Austria by President Ulysses S. Grant. In Vienna, he happened upon a book by Sir John Lubbock, entitled *Prehistoric Times*. Jay was dumbfounded by one of its illustrations, a woodcut of a large rough stone which rested upon three smaller stones and which was described as a "Danish dolmen" but which looked to Jay exactly like the great granite boulder of North Salem.

At the time of Jay's tenure in Austria, many western Europeans were taking an intense interest in some of the ancient artifacts of their past, the large stone structures known as dolmens, cromlechs, and table stones. These, they were discovering, had been erected thousands of years before for burial, religious, and, as is now thought, astronomical purposes. Exposed to this interest, Jay, not surprisingly, came to the conclusion that the North Salem rock and these European stone structures had been built by the same "race which seems to have occupied both continents and to have practiced the same rude architecture for the self-same purpose." When he returned home, he called for an international Congress on prehistoric times to look into this common past.

Jay wasn't successful in arousing enough interest for a Congress, but the idea that America's first European visitors arrived a thousand or more years ago—at least five hundred years before Columbus—has been around ever since. Just which Europeans depends on who you ask—and when. Over the years, Vikings, Irish Culdee monks, Phoenician sailors, Portuguese explorers, and ancient Celts have all been popular candidates with those who believe in "precolonial contact" and have all been the focus of one or more books on the subject.

In the mid-1800s, for instance, New England was swept up in a Viking craze. Certain that the Vikings had sailed as far south as New England, New Englanders turned Leif Ericsson into a local folk hero, and Yankee farmers began to regularly report finding rune stones—stones inscribed with Viking symbols—in their fields. On close examination, these turned out to be run-of-the-mill field stones with a few more glacial scratches than usual; but the Viking craze fueled poems, modern-day sagas, myths, and studies before it died down. Longfellow was inspired to write his narrative poem "A Skeleton

Weighing some sixty tons, the North Salem boulder in North Salem, New York, rests on four small limestone stones and is made of a type of granite said to be found only in New Hampshire and parts of Canada. The boulder has been arousing the curiosity of the area's denizens since at least the 1790s, and today, residents seem more divided than ever as to its origins. While there used to be a sign identifying the boulder as an Ice Age relic, that has recently been replaced by one which fails to even mention the Ice Age and which states in part that "history continues to abound with theories concerning the origin of this massive boulder" and encourages "interested citizens to examine the various facets of current theories."

in Armor" by the discovery of a skeleton garbed in what looked like corroded metal plates in Fall River, Massachusetts. The skeleton turned out to be that of an Algonquin Indian wearing copper jewelry, but in the poem it was transformed into that of a Norse warrior.

Another surge of interest came in the 1930s when Hartford insurance man William Goodwin became convinced that the extensive network of stone walls and stone structures on the piece of property now known as "Mystery Hill" in New Hampshire had been built around 1000 A.D. by monks of an ancient Scoto-Irish order—Culdee monks—and wrote a book about his theory, *The Ruins of Greater Ireland in New England*. The most recent surge occurred in the 1970s when Harvard University professor Barry Fell claimed to have found ancient Celtic inscriptions on the surfaces of glacial erratics and on the stone chambers and granite slabs of "Mystery Hill." This was also the period in which the discovery that Stonehenge was an ancient observatory led American dolmen-believers to reexamine New England stone structures and stone walls, especially walls with upright or standing stones in them, with an eye towards their astronomical significance. Throughout the Northeast, various believers of these theories began studying Ogam, the written language of the ancient Celts, and passing the nights of the summer and winter solstices in root cellars and under glacial erratics, waiting to see the first rays of light as they passed over a purposefully placed rock. Archaeologists and historians looked into the claims that were being made, but always with the same results—inscriptions were found to be plough marks or glacial scratches; the remains associated with these purportedly ancient European sites always proved to be either historical (i.e., colonial or postcolonial) or Indian in nature.

ROSLYN STRONG, A retired designer who now heads the 350-member New England Antiquities Research Association (NEARA) is one of many people in the last century and a half who have been struck by the great resemblance between the stonework and large, perched rocks of New England and the ancient structures and cultural features found throughout northern Europe. Strong, like the others, is convinced that this is not a case of nature imitating art——of glaciers randomly setting down a large number of boulders, a few of which bear an uncanny resemblance to man-made structures elsewhere in the world. Rather, these structures resemble each other because they were built by the same people. And if they were built by the same people, she reasons, then it follows that Europeans must have voyaged to and settled the North American continent long before Columbus's visit.

But Strong is less concerned with who might have settled New England than with documenting the sites they left behind. She feels that the evidence for precolonial settlements is conclusive (but ignored by establishment archaeologists because they do not want to rock the boat of accepted dogma); however, she doesn't know who was responsible. "The longer that I'm involved in this work, the more questions I have and the fewer answers," says Strong, a silver-haired, stylishly dressed woman in her sixties.

Strong adopted the state of Maine seventeen years ago and now makes her home in Wiscasset the base for her study of what she believes to be our precolonial European past. She devotes most of her time to this work; every table and chair in her house is covered with boxes of slides, NEARA publications, computer printouts, and books with titles like *Earlier Than You Think* and *America B.C.* Her garage is full of an exhibit that NEARA put on the year before. Even as a child, she was fascinated by early human history (she remembers wanting to know what happened before the Romans, before the Greeks, and thinking that the Museum of Natural History was by far the best place to go on a Sunday). And today, she gives the impression that she would drop everything at a moment's notice to go look at an unusual wall, a newly discovered stone chamber, or a perched rock.

Maine doesn't have as many stone chambers or perched rocks as do Vermont, Massachusetts, Connecticut, and Rhode Island, so Roslyn Strong and her NEARA colleagues in Maine are concentrating on looking for stone piles with a possible archeoastronomical significance——those that may have been placed by someone to line up with important astronomical events. They distinguish these piles from the garden variety, field clearing piles that one finds everywhere in New England, by the fact that they are located in places that Strong calls "totally out of place for farming" and by the fact that some of the piles have actually been laid rather than heaped together and therefore were "obviously made to last." Others contain what Strong calls a "significantly placed piece of quartz," a mineral believed by some to have healing and other powers.

Piles that fit this bill have been located in Edgecomb and Waldeboro, Maine, and Strong and her co-adventurers have braved poison ivy, ticks, and snakes to survey them with their two-way radios and electronic range finders. After entering their data into a computer and obtaining a printout of the locations of the piles, they use pencils, rulers, and a table of known solar and lunar angles and alignments to determine if any three piles line up with an astronomical event. Not too surprisingly, they sometimes do. Their work seems meticulous, but it lacks certain key elements: random controls (how often would randomly placed dots line up with the rising or setting of any number of stars or planets?) and an awareness of what colonial and postcolonial life was like. Farmers in those days worked pieces of land that we would consider unusable today. And some of them built their rock piles almost as well as their walls for practical reasons: so that they wouldn't occupy more land than necessary or tumble down on the crops around them. Think, too, of the many different ways that people have of stacking wood. Also missing from the chain of reasoning is the fact that quartz is probably the most common mineral in New England. Its presence in rock piles is more likely to be a reflection of its abundance than, as Strong would suggest, ancient mining for quartz.

Strong became president of NEARA in 1985, and she now presides over its membership, the publication of its newsletters and a twice-yearly journal that contains articles with titles like "Stenay: Ritual Murder and Sacred Geometry," and such additions as a New England stone features map, showing the distribution of New England's supposedly ancient artifacts. One of the starred points on this map is "Mystery Hill" in North Salem, New Hampshire, a site whose name has recently been changed to "America's Stonehenge" with a concomitant increase in visitors. Each year 15,000 people visit this site; it includes hundreds of feet of stone walls in which there are many standing

White pines tower over one of the stone chambers of Mystery Hill, New Hampshire. Renamed "America's Stonehenge" by its current owner, the site has been the subject of much theorizing, investigation, and restoration since it was bought in the 1930s by Hartford insurance man William Goodwin.

stones——stones that resemble those at the ancient sites of Avesbury in England and that dolmen-believers say are not typical of farm-wall construction—— several stone cellars or huts, and the remains of a number of other stone structures or chambers that were built on a huge outcropping of granite and constructed with great slabs of granite, slabs weighing four to eleven tons each. The site has undergone conversion and demolition over the years and at various times has been thought to have been built by Goodwin's Irish Cundee monks, by American Indians for religious purposes, by Celts, or by Jonathan Pattee, the nineteenth-century occupant of the site.

Also on NEARA's stone features map are numerous other stone chambers, some of which were exhaustively scrutinized by Giovanna Neudorfer, the state archaeologist of Vermont, in her excellent study published in 1980 of the origins of Vermont's stone chambers. In it, she concludes that, "while there are still many archaeological puzzles in Vermont, the stone chambers are not among them" since "Vermont stone chambers were demonstrably built as root cellars and for other purposes and...fit comfortably into the historic milieu...."

The map is also dotted with numerous other standing stones. "Keep your eyes out for walls with standing stones in them," Roslyn Strong told me. "When you see a standing stone, you often find other things, too." Later, I did just that and was soon noticing standing stones at almost every turn, in walls that I must have passed a hundred times before. But instead of thinking of all the people who could have erected those stones and of all the possible religious or astronomical significances, I found myself pondering the very practical reasons for putting standing stones in a wall. How well worth the effort of pulling a big stone into place and hoisting it upright to know that at least that three-by-four foot section of wall would never have to be rebuilt, that at least there no sheep would ever nudge off a top rock and escape.

Yes, these rocks do resemble those at Avesbury and other sites in England (in shape at least, not always in size; the standing stones at Avesbury, for example, are enormous), but it doesn't follow that they were erected by the same people. As Neudorfer says about stone chambers, "Physical similarities in methods of building construction do not prove a direct relationship between

Sitting alone in a field in Connecticut, this handsome beehive of stone is an example of unusual stonework with a somewhat ordinary explanation. It was built not by Europeans who voyaged to New England a thousand or more years ago, but rather by a hired man in the 1920s. It was a monument to himself, and the field in which it stands has since been known as Monument Pasture.

the builders. . . . " She goes on to quote from another study on prehistoric man in the New World by anthropologist Betty Meggars which notes that "people living in similar kinds of environments, having similar needs for protection from the elements and possessing comparable degrees of technological skill and comparable availability of raw material, are likely to stumble upon similar methods of solving problems of survival." The problem is somewhat akin to that of parallel evolution in biology. Birds, bats, and some squirrels all have flying mechanisms—not because they are closely related but because they all take advantage of similar habitats.

While reflecting on these theories of precolonial contact, it is easy to become increasingly resentful of the idea—implicit in the thinking of Strong and many others—that large stones could be moved about by ancient peoples for religious or astronomical purposes, but not by farmers for pragmatic reasons. "These people really knew what they were doing" is a phrase one often hears in relation to the supposedly ancient peoples who built stone structures. Imbedded in this phrase is the implication that the colonists and postcolonists were incapable of building things that lasted. Absent from it is the awareness that what manages to survive through long periods of time is always that which has been built by people "who knew what they were doing."

The truth of this had been brought home the day before interviewing Roslyn Strong in Wiscasset, when my husband and I spent the morning with Derek Owen, a New Hampshire stone mason. Owen, a gnomish-looking man with two missing fingers—a hazard of his trade—and a long handlebar mustache, gives directions, naturally enough, using stone walls as landmarks. "Take a left at the road where there's a lot of new stonework," he told me over the phone. He went on to describe the new wall. "The stones are pretty small but it doesn't look too bad."

When we arrived, Owen took us on a tour of Hopkinton, New Hampshire, and later of the house that he and his large, extended family live in—a frame house that dates back to the 1850s. All the time, we talked about stone work and what it means to know what you're doing when you are working with stone.

Owen wasn't terribly impressed by the huge granite slabs that were used in the construction of "America's Stonehenge." He had moved a one-ton piece of granite all by himself and took us down into his basement to show it to us. It was a four-by-six-foot granite slab that served as the foundation for a new section of his home. It lay on top of a dry stone wall; the monstrous slab seemed almost to float on the mortarless wall below it, bearing a great resemblance to the type of construction at America's Stonehenge. Owen's basement, in fact, looked very much like that site—except that Owen's basement had a frame house sitting on top of it. But so, at one time, had "America's Stonehenge": the house built by Jonathan Pattee which had burned in 1855, leaving only its stone underbelly.

Also in his basement, Owen showed us what might be one of the apogees of stone construction—a thirty-four-foot deep well lined entirely with glacier-tumbled stones that looked very much like two-foot long, granite eggs, the most unlikely objects with which to build a well. Any well must be able to withstand the pressure of the earth pushing in from every direction. In this particular well, all the withstanding is done by tier upon tier of these egg-shaped stones, each of which has an enormous tendency to pop out of its place. And if even one stone was to go, the entire well might follow. We were looking at the accomplishment of someone who had known what he was doing, but here it was the well of just one house, in one small town in New Hampshire.

Owen had his own explanation for the fact that the stone piles one finds in the woods or fields today are often about twelve feet apart. "Some people think these piles are the remains of Indian villages or ancient civilizations," he told us, "but if you stop to think about it, if you were standing at some point in a field picking the rocks out of the ground, six feet is about the distance that you could throw them."

One of the things that is so interesting about this—more interesting, perhaps, than the question of whether or not there were widespread European settlements in North America predating the ones we know about—is how quickly the commonplace things that people do, things so mundane that people don't even think to document them, become mysteries when the conditions under which these things were first done change. Consider the gypsy moth infestations of several years ago. During those infestations, many homeowners took to putting sticky bands of burlap around their trees to prevent the gypsy moth caterpillar from getting to the leaves. Imagine now that gypsy moths were suddenly to become extinct. What would future generations make of the black rings left by those sticky bands? Or what if the technology for handling garbage was to suddenly change? What would people four hundred years from now infer from the piles of carefully separated bottles and cans that they might find? There's no doubt in my mind that there would be those who would find religious significance in these, the most secular aspects of our lives today.

Similarly, the presence of piles of stones and stone walls on land that looks unfarmable to us began to take on a different aspect soon after the West was opened up to settlement and farmers began abandoning their rocky plots in the East for more fertile ground. Large stone chambers took on a mysterious hue after silos and the ensilage system of producing winter feed for cattle replaced the older method of storing root crops to use as winter fodder. Strong and other believers in precolonial contact describe the stone chambers of New England as "too large" to have been intended for food storage. Salvatore Michael Trento, the author of *The Search for Lost America: Mysteries of the Stone Ruins of the United States*, estimated that just ten chambers located on a one-and-a-half-mile span of roadway in New York were large enough to hold food for 1,755 people— more than the entire population of the area. But Trento and others seem unaware that the chambers stored food for humans but mostly for animals. Animals cannot be maintained through the winter on dry hay alone. Before the introduction of the silo and the concept of ensilage in the 1880s, there was no way of storing corn as fodder. Farmers provided their animals with succulent winter feed by raising root crops—turnips, rutabagas, and mangel-wurtzel (a large beet) and storing them in stone chambers. These chambers were carefully built and oriented to the south or the east—not so as to align with the Celtic solar year but so that the roots inside the cellar would not freeze during the winter months. Farmers of the nineteenth century, it is clear from written historical records, knew to orient their ice houses and dairies to the north and their root cellars and piggeries to the south. And the root cellars were large——not to accommodate all the members of a religious sect but to store the prodigious quantities of roots that a farmer's stock required to bring it through the winter. A single young sheep ate twenty to twenty-three pounds of turnips daily; an oxen, forty pounds.

Scientists have a law, or perhaps it could be called a rule of thumb, that is very useful in distinguishing between all the possible explanations for a given event. It is called the law of parsimony, and it applies here. It says that when there are two or more possible explanations for a single phenomenon, the simplest one is always the more likely, and it is illustrated by the following case. A man wearing a hat is walking down the street when three children appear and begin throwing snowballs at him. The man's hat falls to the ground. An observer might believe that the hat fell because it was knocked off the man's head by a snowball or that it fell because a band of angels swooped down and took it off the man's head. The law of parsimony would state that the first explanation is the simplest and, therefore, the most probable. In the question of how large rocks came to be resting on sets of smaller stones and who built New England's stone chambers, scientists see the glaciers and colonial settlers as the children throwing snowballs; the ancient Celts, Irish monks, or Phoenician sailors as the bands of angels. Roslyn Strong and other NEARA members do not agree, but they may have other reasons for wanting to believe in their theories, reasons that may have much to do with their beliefs that ancient man was much more in touch with the earth and the stars than his modern counterpart and that establishment archaeologists have conspired to keep us from learning the truth about our past.

In the end, a good theory has to account for all of the facts, not just some of them. It has to be probable and not just possible. Ancient settlement hypotheses are certainly theoretically possible and they do offer one account for the existence of similar stone structures in New England and Europe. But they fail to explain why excavations of these structures have never turned up anything other than historic or late Indian remains. And is it reasonable to believe that a civilization which had the manpower and wherewithal to move a sixty-ton piece of rock could inhabit New England yet leave nothing behind, no cooking utensils, no tools or pottery, no bone fragments or other remains, nothing except the rock itself? Or are those who advocate those theories just imagining angels?

The theories of ancient settlements also fail to explain another tragic but

A farm boy and his oxen standing in front of a large pile of rutabagas——one of several different kinds of roots used by farmers throughout most of the nineteenth century as winter feed for their livestock. Farmers grew prodigious quantities of these roots because their livestock consumed so much (one oxen, for example, might eat forty pounds of roots per day), and they stored them in large stone root cellars where they would remain fresh and nutritious throughout the cold months. Now that silos and ensilage have replaced root cellars and root crops, some people have found it easy to forget about this chapter in American agriculture and have assigned new meanings and origins to those cellars they find in the woods.

cogent fact. It is well known that when the Pilgrims and Puritans first arrived in this country, they found and settled the sites of numerous, recently abandoned Indian villages—a circumstance that had much to do with the success of the early settlements since the settlers could plant corn and cut hay without having to go through the laborious process of clearing the land. Demographic and medical historians now realize that the reason these villages were deserted was because the Indians who had inhabited them had been decimated by diseases that they had picked up from contact with the earliest European explorers, hunters, and fishermen: chicken pox, measles, small pox, influenza, malaria, yellow fever, and tuberculosis. In the first seventy years of the seventeenth century, it is estimated that the Indian population of New England fell from more than seventy thousand to less than twelve thousand. Puritans took this decimation, this "sweeping away great multitudes of the natives ... that he might make room for us there" as a sure sign that it was God's wish that the new land be theirs; but it had a much more natural explanation.

For hundreds of generations, American Indians had been separated from their ancestors on the Asian continent, and during that time they had lived remarkably healthy lives, free of the diseases that were a constant in the lives of Asians and Europeans. This had been a blessing for thousands of years but in the sixteenth and seventeenth centuries, it backfired. The Indians had been, as historian Neal Salisbury puts it, "hermetically sealed from the immunities that had been established in the Eastern Hemisphere over the previous 40,000 years" and as such they constituted a vast "virgin soil" for the disease pools of Europeans. When these diseases were introduced in the late sixteenth and early seventeenth centuries, the effect was quick and devastating.

The question for those who believe in precolonial settlement of New England by Europeans is this: if the native Indians of New England had been having continuous contact with Europeans over thousands of years, as they suggest, how is it they did not acquire an immunity to European diseases? How is it that they were suddenly so ravaged by those diseases in the sixteenth and seventeenth centuries?

But beliefs, as everyone knows, are not about facts, and the conviction that Europeans inhabited New England long before the colonists is sure to revive from time to time. Apparently, many find this a much more intriguing possibility than either the facts of the Ice Age or the documented history of this country. Meanwhile, those of us who are doubters can get excited by imagining that the places in New England and New York where we now live and work were once covered with ice a mile thick. It can make one feel incredibly small. It makes even the rock at North Salem, the beginning of so much speculation, seem small, for in an ice sheet a mile thick, a rock the size of the North Salem boulder is as a pebble only an inch long in a stream eight feet deep. Yet, who would ever wonder if such a pebble was found perched on three smaller stones, or if such a pebble lined up with the summer solstice?

PART III

WALLING IN THE LAND

6

A FRENZY OF WALL BUILDING

AMID the many, enduring questions about the stone walls and stone structures of New England and New York, one thing is known for certain: numerous factors combined to make the years between 1775 and 1825 the most active period of wall building that this area has ever experienced.

One of these factors, the progressive deforestation of New England during the colonial and postcolonial years, has already been mentioned. Despite the warnings of some, most New Englanders had a definitively non-conservationist approach to their timber resources. Yet, they were taken by surprise at how soon those resources were depleted. The Revolutionary War exacerbated an already critical situation, and after the war many farmers found themselves having to rebuild fences that had been burned for fuel and homes that had been destroyed in battle, but with very little timber available. For fences, at least, stone provided a time-consuming, but long-lasting alternative. Stone walls also had another advantage, shared only by worm or zig-zag fencing. In some parts of New England and New York, bedrock is so close to the surface that it makes digging holes for fence posts impossible. Many early farmers, therefore, never even had the option of turning to such less timber-extravagent forms of fencing as post and rail.

In 1789, when George Washington toured the area around Rye, New York, he noted that "the farms are very close together, and separated, as one

Though the majority of New England's stone walls were built in the period following the American Revolution, walls were common features of the landscape even before then. During the Revolution, they played a role as bunkers, deflecting both rebel and English bullets. "I saw ther Byonets over the Growing Corn, and wee three in number lay In ambush in a very safe place," noted John Hempstead in his account of the events of The Battle of Groton Heights, "& the Enemy advancing in an Indian file, they advansed to a Stone Wall that coverd our left hand." In this illustration of the British marching into Concord, Massachusetts (taken from the engraving by Amos Doolittle), troops are lined up outside the walls of the town's cemetery or burying ground.

enclosure after another also is, by fences of stone, which are indeed easily made, as the country is immensely stoney." What he did not mention was that these stone fences had just recently taken the place of the worm fences that had prevailed in this region before the war.

A second reason for the boom of wall building during this period was the end of the practice of common herding and the enclosure of previously common lands. Farmers had long questioned this vestige of English agriculture on account of its inconvenience and waste. Because common lands often lay at some distance from a farmer's barns, much time was spent bringing animals to and from the fields; and valuable land had to be used not for crops but for the numerous roads by which each proprietor gained access to his particular allotments. By the end of the eighteenth century, however, farmers began to wonder whether common herding constituted good husbandry. When stock ran in common, it was impossible for an individual farmer to improve his particular cattle or sheep through selective breeding. Also, his land did not benefit from the manuring that enclosed stock would give it.

In a spirit of improvement, many common fields came to be divided up and fenced individually—often with stone walls. As with earlier fencing, these divisions were made under the reigning assumption that small fields produce best. "Where there are more [stones] than is needed," the 1790 *New England Farmer or Georgical Dictionary* advised, "the walls may be thicker and higher than is needful on other accounts; and lots fhould be made the fmaller; for there are certain conveniences in having fmall fixed lots...."

Even though small fields required more fencing than large ones (a field of ten acres, for example, requires sixteen rods of fence per acre while one of a hundred acres requires less than a third of that) New Englanders readily embraced this advice. They, who looked upon fencing as the most visible sign of an improved landscape, turned New England into a patchwork of small, walled enclosures. As George Waring, a nineteenth-century agricultural writer observed, "there are whole townships [in New England and southern New York] in which the fields will not average two acres in extent. I think I have seen farms in which they average less than one acre."

Perhaps the most important spur to wall building at the end of the eighteenth century was a sudden increase in the popularity of sheep raising. Up until the American Revolution, sheep raising on a large scale had been confined to New England's coast and offshore islands—areas that afforded both protection from predators and the wide marshes and grasslands in which sheep, picky eaters that they are, like to browse. In 1773, Nantucket with 15,000 sheep and Martha's Vineyard with 20,000 were essentially two vast sheep pastures, as were many other islands. Then, political developments and a series of setbacks shifted sheep farming to the mainland.

First, many of the offshore islands lost most of their flocks to the British, during the Revolutionary War and again during the War of 1812. Then after the Revolution, local governments on the mainland, which were short on cash but dependent on expensive wool imports, began to provide farmers with inducements to promote the raising of sheep. Some towns gave farmers tax incentives; others required all able-bodied men to work one day a year clearing brush in order to create pastureland suitable for sheep. After the War of 1812, Congress enacted the first tariff law designed to protect American manufactures and farm products; this law, along with others that followed, provided the basis on which farmers in many parts of New England abandoned dairying and grain raising and filled their pastures with sheep. In some towns, this switch happened so suddenly that families found themselves without enough grain to make bread.

But sheep farming and wool manufacturing got its biggest boost in 1811 when William Jarvis, the U.S. consul in Lisbon, requested and finally received permission to purchase 200 of the prized wool-bearing Merino rams from the Spanish royal flocks, flocks that had previously been jealously guarded. In the eighteenth century, New England had basically just two different breeds of sheep; since neither was particularly noted for its fleece, Jarvis's coup was a matter of great importance. In 1811, Jarvis shipped his prize sheep to Weathersfield, Vermont; and as the blood of the Merinos spread so did the profits of sheep raising. In 1812, the average fleece of a sheep in Vermont was only six percent of the animal's live weight; by 1844, it was fifteen percent; and by 1865, twenty-one percent.

This emphasis on breeding was paralleled by a surge in fencing and wall building. In the newer settlements of Vermont and New Hampshire, where much of the land had never known the plow and timber was still available, sheep fencing tended to be made of posts and rails. "Farmers only moved

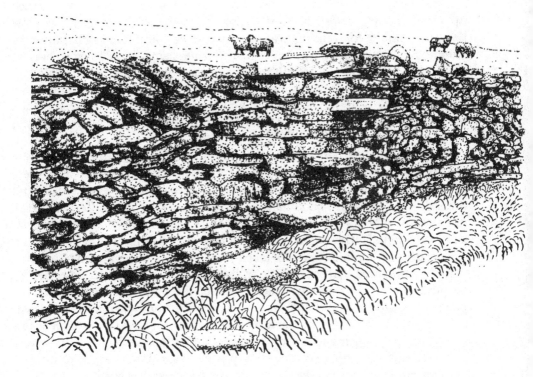

As farmers walled in their fields for sheep, they needed ways to get from one pasture into another. Stiles provided inexpensive and reliable (unlike gates, they always stayed shut) shortcuts between fields and were constructed in a wide variety of ways. This cantilevered step stile is a tour de force requiring careful construction and large flat stones.

stones when they plowed a field," Jane Dorney, a geographer who has examined the agricultural land-use patterns of the Green Mountains of Vermont, once told me. "So in Vermont where only a small proportion of the land had been cultivated, most sheep fencing was made of wood."

In southern New England, by contrast, farmers fenced many of their new sheep pastures in stone. Most of this pasture land had been converted from some other agricultural use, and two hundred years of cultivation had turned up an abundant supply of stone. Also, in many parts of southern New England, timber for fencing was just not to be had. Manasseh Miner, of Stonington, Connecticut, was one of many farmers who began to raise sheep in the 1820s. In 1826, he acquired thirty-five animals and turned much of his 240-acre farm into a warren of small enclosures, each of which he surrounded by a wall about five feet high. Many of the walls still exist today (though the tax records of Stonington show that Miner got out of the sheep business in 1831, just six years after he had entered it).

Though it is certain that many nineteenth-century farmers fenced their sheep pastures with stone, it is not at all certain how effective these walls were at actually confining these agile animals. That seems to have depended on both the wall—on its height and quality—and the breed of sheep. "A poor fence makes an unruly animal and a good fence an orderly one," it used to be said. One postcolonial farmer noted that "a stone wall of five feet is a better security against unruly animals than a rail fence of seven"; but observers from the same period complained that most stone walls appeared to be "tossed together for no purpose but to afford the quadrapeds of the place the means of taking practical lessons in the art of jumping." The stone wall, when well made, was probably the best of all possible fences, but when poorly made—as it seems many walls were—it was one of the worst. It was thrown down every winter and needed to be repaired, not merely every year, but every spring when farmers were at their busiest. As George Waring once observed,

> Probably the majority of the stone walls in New England commenced their
> career as a tier of boulders and irregular stones set one above the other, on

the surface of the ground, and kept in position by a very nice adjustment of their centers of gravity; and such of them as were without yearly care have ended it as long heaps of rubbish, covered with brambles and elder bushes,——a sort of spontaneous hedge with a stone foundation, flanked by thistles, cockles, ironweed, and golden rod;——possessing all the disadvantages and performing few of the offices of a fence.

Bernice Wing describes just such fences on her grandfather's farm in Vermont——"old stone walls topped with poles, with brush for filling gaps"——and outlines their problems. "In the middle of the summer," Wing wrote in *A Vermont Sketchbook: Memories of a Vermont Quaker Farm*, "brush fences revealed their inadequacies: they became a nuisance at many needy points. By that time adventurous members of the flock had found all the loopholes and were leading their fellows wherever they would."

And stone walls, it appears, needed to be particularly well built in order to deter sheep for, unlike other animals, sheep will constantly test a wall, looking for a gap, for loose stones which they can nudge to the ground and set them on their way in their search for greener pastures. Once a flock of sheep has acquired the habit of jumping fences, farmers agree, it is a very difficult one to break. A conscientious farmer made sure that his sheep didn't acquire it in the first place——by building stout, high walls.

What constitutes a sufficiently high fence to keep in sheep? Most towns, as noted, required fences from four and a half to five feet high. Those stone walls that were built to a height of only three feet were then topped with rails, riders, or brush to give them the additional height. In areas where stone was particularly abundant, the walls themselves might be very thick and at least five feet high. In *The Book of the Farm*, published in 1852, Henry Stephens contends that a stone wall five quarters (four feet nine inches) in height, "will fence horses and cattle, and Leicester sheep, but will not confine black-faced sheep." The black-faced sheep, one of New England's two early breeds, was a long-legged sheep distantly related to today's Hampshires and to the extremely nimble Scottish blackfaces, and they required a higher wall.

Wandering sheep were so great a problem for the farmers of the nineteenth century that at least one farmer——frustrated at his unsuccessful efforts at keeping his sheep from jumping fences——tried instead to breed jumping out of his sheep. The result was the "otter sheep," a breed of "good flesh" with short legs that bowed outwards like those of an otter. These sheep must have been horrible to look at, but they did not jump fences, and in Connecticut, Massachusetts, and Rhode Island in the early nineteenth century, the breed was very popular.

At the same time that New England farmers were beginning to convert their wheat fields to sheep pastures, a development was taking place in the towns of New England that would eventually transform the nature of farming in the region, as well as contribute to the nineteenth century's wall-building boom. This was the growth of manufacturing. Or, rather, not so much the growth of manufacturing itself, but the growth of an industrial or manufacturing population——a population that needed the goods that farmers produced.

Before the nineteenth century, farming in New England was largely a self-sufficient affair. Unlike the tobacco farmer of Virginia and the rice, cotton, and indigo farmers of Georgia and the Carolinas, the seventeenth and eighteenth century farmers of New England had no defined market for their products. Trading among farmers did take place (in services as well as goods; one eighteenth-century farmer might build a wall for his neighbor in exchange for a quantity of wheat or hay; another might transport wheat or rye to a region where prices for those goods were high); but, by and large, the entire population was agricultural and produced much the same products. Before 1810, each farmer divided his land into the same proportions of woodland, pasturage, and tillage and raised much the same crops and the same proportions of different kinds of stock. There was little specialization as each farmer was trying to raise or make most of what his family needed. Cash was a rare commodity, and it was used to buy salt, sugar, iron, and maybe liquor.

Then in the first half of the nineteenth century, an industrial revolution took place in the eastern states. Power machinery came to replace hand tools, and many of the processes of manufacturing were transferred from the farmhouse to the factory. When manufacturing split from agriculture a specialized, nonagricultural class arose, a class that consumed——rather than produced——farm products. The demographics of the area turned around. In 1810, in Massachusetts, Rhode Island, and Connecticut combined, there were only three towns with as many as 10,000 inhabitants: Boston, Providence, and New Haven. Together, those three towns had a population of 56,000, less than seven percent of the population total. By 1860, the same three states had over twenty-six towns with ten thousand inhabitants or more each, for a total of 682,000 people or 36.5 percent of the total population of southern New England.

Historians say that it is impossible to overestimate the effect that the growth of this market had on the area's agriculture. It encouraged both progress and differentiation. The home market gave incentive to farmers to raise those things for which their farms were best suited. Farms near industrial towns——those near the mill towns of Fall River, New Bedford, and New Haven, and within a market radius of New York and Boston, for instance——came to specialize in dairy farming and market gardening, raising onions, carrots, turnips, and potatoes. Those farms located at a greater distance from the population centers specialized according to the vagaries of their natural resources. In northern Massachusetts, many farmers turned exclusively to the fattening of beef cattle, while in hilly areas throughout New England, they devoted themselves to wool growing, clearing the hilltops of Vermont and New Hampshire almost to their summits. Farms in Massachusetts and Connecticut that lay along the Connecticut River were turned over to the cultivation of tobacco.

The home market led to an influx of cash into these previously cash-starved farms; this cash was in turn used to improve the farms and the life of the farm family in general. In 1837, the Reverend John Kelly of Hamstead, a small town in New Hampshire, was among those who observed the remarkable changes that were taking place, changes that were reiterated in town after town throughout New England. "The meeting house was all tattered and torn," this pastor noted,

without a steeple, without a bell, and almost without a covering; and might have remained so for an age, or till it rotted down, if it had not been for the people of God, who, with their own money and hands, by divine aid, put it in a better condition. The roads were full of stones, or in some places of mire; but now for almost six miles, they are paved underneath with stone, and covered with gravel. The buildings, which were mostly old and shattered, are now repaired or replaced for new ones, and many new and handsome houses are reared up where there were none before. The fences, reeling and decaying, are turned into stone wall, of which perhaps, there is more than in any other town of the same size.

Wealth brought a spirit of improvement to farming: depleted soils were renewed, fences rebuilt, the breeds of stock improved, and farmers were able to invest in new pieces of equipment such as the iron plow. Another sign of the times was the emergence of agricultural societies and the publication of farming magazines. In 1811, Elkanal Watson founded the first American agricultural society; by 1857, New England had ninety-five of them. The publication of *The American Farmer* and the *Plough Boy* in 1819 marked the beginning of agricultural journalism in this country, and it wasn't long before those publications were joined by *The New England Farmer, The Maine Farmer, The Cultivator, The Farmer's Monthly Visitor,* and *The Farmer's Companion,* among others.

These publications offered farmers advice on every aspect of farming—from the culturing of silk worms to the manuring of fields—and their pages were filled with advice on building fences and homilies about fencing, with such sayings as:

Land which is not worth fencing is not worth having.

For every stone which you pick up and move you shall have a credit; for every valuable tree which you cut down you shall have a debt.

If a poor farmer happens to have a good fence it is good luck, but it is considered an indispensable item for a good farmer to have a good fence.

The introduction of fences into agriculture was about as great an improvement in the progress of that art, as that of the practice of the division of labour into the art of manufacture.

In 1845, *The Farmer's Monthly Visitor* (a publication "intended to promote the interest of the farmer; to defend the dignity of the agricultural profession, and encourage the practice of domestic economy") told its readers to "take another look at your enclosures and see that your fences are sound firm, high and close. If you do not, and should unhappily wake up some morning and find your cattle in the corn, your pigs in the peas, &c., you will please to recollect that we told you so."

And in 1842, *The Cultivator* (whose stated purpose was "to improve the soil and the mind") reminded farmers that "good fences prevent eructations of bile among neighbors (a less poetic way of saying, "good fences make good neighbors"), contribute much to the good appearance of the farm, prevent the destruction of crops, and check in the bud that disposition to live at large which exists in most animals."

Most of the publications also advised their readers that it was wise to replace their "half rotted, worm eaten fences" with stone walls and that when building those walls, they should spend the time and money to build them well. But when it comes time to offer practical advice on how best to build a stone wall, these publications, curiously enough, almost always disagree in nearly every aspect of construction. While one might strongly advocate that every wall should have a foundation that extends all the way down to the frost line, another suggests that if the proposed site for a wall is level, or nearly so, no further preparation is necessary. A third recommends digging down only as far as hardpan or unbroken ground and laying a foundation just several inches deep.

These agricultural periodicals do concur that flat stones are the easiest type to lay and that walls made with flat rectangular slabs tend to withstand the heaving of frost better than those made of rounded field stones. But given a farmer who has only field stones, one publication advised that he lay the biggest of those stones at the base of the wall, while another suggested saving the biggest stones for the top (to weigh down the wall) and using the small stones on the bottom (to absorb the movement of the earth). Still another advised farmers to build walls with only the very largest stones that they could dig out of the earth since a wall made of very massive blocks won't be moved

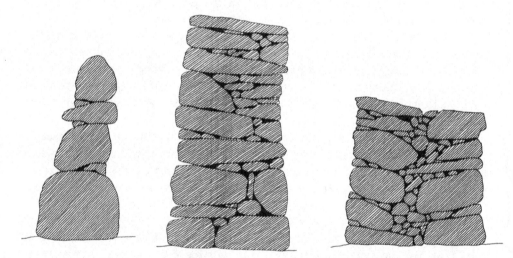

Cross sections of a few of New England's early wall types. Many farmers surrounded their fields with walls that lacked a foundation and were simply arrangements of stones, a single layer thick (left), but they put more time and energy into those walls around their barnyard and gardens. These walls might have a foundation extending down to below the frostline. The style of their construction would vary according to the type of stone available and the skill and training of the builder. A laid wall (middle), a wall in which every stone is carefully tied and chinked into place, is best made with a good proportion of large, well-shaped stones. A rubble wall (right), on the other hand, can be made with stones of every shape and size. It is built like a sandwich, with two outer layers of larger stones and a rubble or small stone filling in between.

by anything, not even the many earthquakes that punctuated postcolonial life. Several of these publications stress the fact that walls with a north-south orientation will survive frost heaves much better than those with an east-west orientation, but they don't say how it is possible to fence in a pasture with walls that only run in one direction.

The letters to the editors in these publications are also filled with suggestions on better ways of building walls. One subscriber to *The Cultivator* wrote in to recommend "a liberal use of sticks" in building a wall to ensure that the stones will lie flat (no mention is made of what happens to the wall when the sticks rot). A reader of *The Farmer's Monthly Visitor* advocated walls made of alternative layers of sod and stone which are then scattered all over with grass seed to give "a most beautiful and solid wall."

In the midst of all these different opinions regarding wall building, there seemed to be only one aspect of the task that every nineteenth-century commentator on wall building was able to agree upon, something so essential that it appears to have been learned early and well by all. That is the importance of "breaking up the joints," laying the stones so that the joints between them do not fall on top of one another, thereby forming a weak or fault line in the wall, a point where the wall would have a tendency to come apart. This is avoided by always laying one stone on top of two stones and two stones on top of one. "One on two and two on one" soon became the first commandment of wall building, as illustrated by the often repeated anecdote about a farmer who wants a stone wall built and advertises for a man to do the job.

When a prospective builder appears, the farmer asks him, "How do you build a stone wall?"

"Why, by laying one stone on another," the jobber replies.

"You won't do for me," the farmer says and sends the wall builder on his way. Another jobber comes, and the farmer asks, "And how do you lay stone wall?"

"I lay one stone on the top of two stones," he answers.

"Very well then," the farmer says, "go to work."

BUT AS FOR every other aspect of wall building, the methods of the nineteenth century were phenomenally diverse. If there is an explanation for this diversity, it must lie, at least in part, in the nature of wall building itself, in the fact that "wall building," as a stone mason today puts it, "is a three-dimensional puzzle with an infinite number of solutions." No two people will build a wall quite the same way; given identical piles of rocks and fifty wall builders, one could wind up with fifty different walls. These walls would, undoubtedly, fall into some basic groupings: double walls (walls made of two thickness of stone), single walls, angled or vertical walls, faced walls (walls with at least one flat side) and double-faced walls, capped walls, and walls with or without a foundation. Yet among these different walls, there might be no single best one. Whether because of climate, topography, luck, or skill, walls of many different kinds manage to stand the test of time. There is a large element of unpredictability to wall building, which even some wall builders acknowledge. "For a while, I was foolish enough to tell people that the wall I was building for them would last for a hundred years," says Derek Owen. "Now that I've had to repair a number of walls that I've built, I'm much more humble."

Another aspect to any explanation of the diversity of wall building techniques must be historical. Wall building in New England in the nineteenth century—like the agricultural journals in which it was discussed—was really in its infancy. In parts of New England, walls had only recently become the fences of choice, so it was not yet known which ways of building a wall would work and which ways wouldn't. Also, in order to learn how to build a wall, New England farmers could not turn to a specialized class of wall builders trained in a long-standing tradition—for until the nineteenth century, there were not many men who specialized in that profession. Rather they had to learn from that infinitely harsher teacher: trial and error. It is this which is reflected in the pages of the agricultural journals of the early nineteenth century. This and the possibility that some editors may have been reluctant to tell their readers that the best and surest ways to build walls—as experience did begin to show—were also the hardest, requiring the digging of deep foundations, the use of large stones, and the capping of the wall with heavy flat stones.

From the plethora of early techniques, two basic types of walls did emerge, but their differences had much more to do with time and effort than style. There were, on the one hand, walls which were built with a great deal of care, laid walls as they were sometimes called; and, on the other hand, thrown walls, those which were put up much more hastily. Many of the walls surrounding fields and marking property lines were of the latter type. Built without a foundation, these walls were simply arrangements of rocks, often a single layer thick, placed directly on the ground, with the smaller rocks (or one-man stones) laid on top of the larger ones (the whoobies or two-man stones). Two men with a yoke of oxen could build a rod of this type of wall a day, it used to be said.

New Englanders tended to put their time and energy into the walls that counted most—the walls around their farmyards, garden plots, town pounds, and cemeteries. These were walls that they wanted to be frostproof, so before they laid them they dug a trench three feet deep or more so that the big foundation stones would lie below the frost line. Then they added the rest of their stones, carefully chinking each one into place with small stones, known in different areas as shims, chinkers, chinks, or chocks, and topping the entire thing off with heavy capping stones.

In the late 1800s, when Haydn Pearson was a boy growing up in Vermont, he spent a summer helping an old wall builder build a wall of this type on a sidehill slope of a farmyard. "We had dug the trench deep and wide," Pearson remembered many years later. "Slowly the wall rose. The old man was very particular about each rock and chinking piece. To an impatient lad, the old craftsman was unconscionably slow. The idea of chinking rocks below the soil surface was particularly tiresome and irksome. 'Who's going to know if these are chinked or not' was a boy's question. The old man's astonishment was genuine as he peered over his spectacles. 'Why,' he said, 'I will—and so will you.'"

7

Wall Builders of Early New England

THE walls of early New England, those thousands and thousands of miles of stone stitching on the landscape, are the handiwork, we know, of innumerable farmers and laborers of the seventeenth, eighteenth, and nineteenth centuries. But try to find out how any one of these farmers or laborers thought about this task, and one is liable to come up with a frustrating lack of information. Wall building, like so many of a farmer's menial jobs, was something that had to be done, not commented on. Except for such frequent but taciturn diary entries as "Hauled stone this aft" or "Laid 10 feet of wall," there is a dearth of written record about the building of stone walls by the people who actually built them. Stone walls are the anonymous epics of earlier generations, lyric forms in rock, which, when they were being composed on the face of the landscape, were never signed and rarely reflected upon——at least in writing.

The lack of written material is interesting in itself, for it shows better than anything in writing ever could how ordinary these enduring objects were once thought to be. Still, when I began to write this book, I hoped and expected to find the letters or diaries of at least one or two articulate wall builders with firsthand descriptions of what it was like to turn New England's confused mass of rocks and trees into fields and fences, to repair the same recalcitrant wall year after year. With all the walls——and, therefore, wall builders——that had once existed, this expectation did not seem unreasonable, though I knew it would require some searching. Yet I succeeded in turning up very little firsthand material, material that would give some idea of the flavor of this back-breaking task. It wasn't until the project was almost finished that I happened upon the recently republished autobiography of Asa Sheldon, farmer, trader, and working man, who was born in 1788 and died in 1870, having acquired some reputation as a teamster (of oxen) and stone mason. Sheldon writes only little about wall building itself, but he gives a very good idea of what it was like to handle oxen and to be a Yankee farmer living by his wits, industriousness, and nose for a good trade.

Sheldon's autobiography aside, part of the lack of material on wall building by wall builders was due to oversight rather than deficit. Because many librarians and curators were not particularly interested in stone walls, they tended to overlook the references to them in their collections. At one New York historical society, endowed with a substantial number of eighteenth- and nineteenth-century account books, the librarian, though extremely helpful, assured me that I would find nothing in those accounts about walls; she had been through them many times and could not recall seeing anything on the subject. We were both somewhat amazed when page after page of these account books and diaries were found to contain references—albeit sparse, nondescriptive ones—to the acts of building walls, drawing stone, fixing fences, and more.

Elsewhere, the same was true of colonial land agreements and fencing agreements; walls and fences were one of their main ingredients and gave a very good indication of when stone walls were being built and, also, which areas had stone to build with. On Martha's Vineyard, for example, stone walls begin to show up in the deeds and agreements of the late 1700s, but only in those from the towns of Chilmark and Tisbury, located in the southeastern part of the island—the only part of the island where the glaciers deposited any stone.

From these account books and diaries, I also discovered some surprising things about the builders of New England's stone walls. These walls had not all been erected by the stalwart Yankee farmer of my imagining, that hard-working, inventive, Jack-of-all-trades, who could, as an admiring Englishman once put it, "mend his plough, erect his walls, thrash his corn, handle his axe, his hoe, his sithe, his saw, break a colt or drive a team, with equal address...." Yankee farmers may have done all of these things, but they also relied on much additional labor. In different areas, at different times (and over the course of centuries of settlement), American Indians, black slaves, and indentured servants also built walls. An entry in an account book, an excerpt from a town record, are the only pieces left to tell about this aspect of American history. But even those few pieces, when put together, cast a new hue on the farm walls of the northern states.

What is well documented are the chronic labor shortages of the colonies. From the beginning, these shortages were an inevitable and serious result of the cheapness of land, the lack of a permanent class of agricultural laborers (as existed in England), and the small amount of overseas immigration from 1675 to 1775. Wealthier settlers often brought indentured servants with them, but others made early attempts to use native Indians as farm laborers. In parts of New England, these attempts did not meet with much success. One colonist, in describing the reasons for this, reveals his own ignorance of traditional Indian divisions of labor and sex roles.

"If one of these savages allows himself to be persuaded by a Christian to work," this man wrote, "he does it with complaining, shame, and fear, as an unaccustomed act; he looks about him all the while on both sides, lest any of his people may find him working, just as if work were a disgrace, and idleness were an especial inborn privilege of the nobility, which should not be soiled by the sweat of the toil."

In other areas, though, colonists came to use Indian labor extensively. Some of the Indians who worked for the settlers were free men who were paid a daily wage, but others were slaves, captives from the King Philip's Indian War of 1675 who had been subsequently awarded to colonists in compensation for their own participation in that war. Both of these groups of Indians were probably employed in building stone walls. In 1677, the missionary Daniel Cookin noted that the Narragansett and Warrick tribes of Connecticut and Rhode Island were "an active, laborious, and ingenious people which is demonstrated in their labors they do for the English of whom more are employed, especially in making stone fences and many other hard labors, than any other Indian people or neighbors."

Much later, the Reverend William Emerson, who wrote about the area of Little Compton, Rhode Island, in the 1800s also observed that "the Indians were remarkable for the excellence of their stone wall and were much employed in this kind of labor."

And in the records of Plymouth are several accounts of Indians building stone walls for colonists to pay off a debt. Most of these exchanges took place in territory which was once part of Massachusetts but is now Rhode Island, and one raises the interesting possibility that Indian women as well as men were responsible for building walls.

On October 20, 1672, the following appears on record in Plymouth: "Whereas Awashonks Sqaw Sachem stands indebted unto Mr. John Almy for the sum of 25 pds to be paid in porke at three pence per pound or peage (wampum) at 16 penny and 20 pole of stone wall at four pds, which stone wall or four pounds is to be understood to be part of the fine.... "

On first reading, it seems that an Indian woman is being asked here to build a stone wall, something that is, in fact, not too unlikely given that Indian women were used to doing much of their people's heavy labor. But Awashonks was a sachem or tribal chief (a position she attained after the death of her husband who had been the sachem), and it is equally possible that the debt that she has been ordered to pay off was not one that she had incurred personally but, rather, one owed by her tribe. In that case, Awashonks might not have been responsible for the actual building of the wall but just for seeing that it was done.

Elsewhere, the building of colonial walls by Indians is not as well documented, but oral history has it that it took place. On Martha's Vineyard, where there is still a large Indian community, many inhabitants have heard that most of the island's stone walls were built by Algonquin Indians, and some say that the Indians were often paid in whiskey.

Employing the native Indians was not the only solution that colonists tried in order to solve their persistent labor problems. The importation of black slaves was another. Though many of us associate slavery only with the southern states, numerous New England farmers kept slaves until well into the eighteenth century. Slavery was not abolished in Connecticut and Rhode Island until 1774 (at which time the descendants of the original Indian slaves were also set free) and in Massachusetts, not until 1781.

In actual numbers, of course, the slave holdings of the northern colonies never compared with those of the South. In 1770, for example, the black population of Maryland alone was 63,818, more than New York and all the New England states combined. In that same year, New York had a population of 19,112 blacks (a number which would have included slaves plus any freemen); Connecticut had 5,698; Massachusetts, 4,754; Rhode Island, 3,761; New Hampshire, 541; Maine, 458; and Vermont, 50.

Northerners were not adverse to keeping slaves, but they never utilized slave labor to the extent that it was used in the South. Historians have established that the reasons for this rested on economic rather than on religious or moral grounds. In some of the first settlements, experiments were made with black and Indian slave labor, but it was soon apparent that the slave system did not yield a profit where farming was done on a subsistence or self-sufficient basis or in order to supply a limited market. And with few exceptions, self-sufficiency was a hallmark of New England farming until well into the nineteenth century. But where these exceptions occurred, in those parts of New England where farming was pursued on a large scale early on (the areas around Rhode Island's Narragansett Bay, for example), slavery was employed extensively.

From the first, southern Rhode Island and parts of eastern Connecticut had been noted for their suitability for large-scale sheep and cattle raising. Later, in the eighteenth century, when most New England farmers were growing only for their family's needs on farms that averaged about 100 acres, Rhode Island farmers were exporting cattle, sheep, and cheese, as well as horses, to the West Indies and tending acreages of a thousand or more. The size of their farms, or plantations as these enormous holdings in the Narragansett Colony were called, was possible only because of the extensive use of slaves as agricultural laborers. In the early years of the eighteenth century, Rhode Island ships started trading with Africa and bringing back slaves. Soon, Rhode Island outdid all the other northern states in proportions of slaves, if not in actual numbers. By the mid-eighteenth century, the town of South Kingstown, for example, had one black person for every three whites.

Almost none of the records or account books from Rhode Island's plantations have survived, so it is difficult to surmise to what extent these slaves were used to build Rhode Island's extensive network of stone walls. However, in one of the very few existing, day-to-day records of slave labor on the Yankee plantation——the diary of Reverand James MacSparran, a landowner in southern Rhode Island in the mid-eighteenth century——the building of one stone wall by a slave is mentioned.

In September 1743, MacSparran noted in his diary that work was started on a wall "to the northward of the north orchard" and that through the following weeks Harry, MacSparran's most valuable slave, was busy digging and "sledding" stones. Tom Walmsley, a neighbor who often hired himself out as a day laborer and who was skilled in the art of stone-wall construction, was employed to aid in the building. According to MacSparran's records, he and Harry very often worked side by side, hoeing corn, pitching hay, and picking peas.

Oral tradition also has it that slaves built many of the walls in parts of Connecticut. Fifty years ago, Harold G. Holcombe interviewed several long-time residents of eastern Connecticut for an article in *The Antiquarian* and learned that these informants had been told by their grandfathers that slaves had built the walls. Slavery reached its peak in Connecticut, Rhode Island, and elsewhere in the mid-eighteenth century, several decades before New England went through its real frenzy of wall building; however, because Rhode Island and eastern Connecticut were settled earlier than other parts of New England (and because they relied on slave labor), they also went through most stages of settlement earlier——including fencing. Also, in parts of eastern Connecticut and southern Rhode Island such as the towns of Aquidneck, Portsmouth, Middletown, and Newport, farmers may have turned almost immediately to stone to solve their fencing needs because the kind of stone that was readily available in those areas——a kind of gneiss——was ideal for wall building. This stone, which looks like slate, breaks off into tabular sheets that almost look as if they have been quarried and produce remarkably neat-looking walls.

In other parts of New England and New York, where subsistence farming was more the rule, some farmers kept slaves to employ in the fields or use as domestic servants—but usually only between two and four. This was especially true in the colonies of Connecticut, Massachusetts, and New York, which also had large slave holdings. Maine, New Hampshire, and Vermont, on the other hand, never had more than about one thousand slaves between them.

Historians have argued as to whether the slaves on most New England farms would have been used for such skilled work as wall building. Some have suggested that slaves were used primarily in the house and for very heavy outdoor work, but the records suggest otherwise. In the relatively few accounts of the colonial period that I've examined, there have been several mentions of slaves building stone walls. The account ledger of Ezekiel Hawley, a Quaker from North Salem, New York, makes note that in 1787 a slave called Robbin was to be given a "Credit for making stone fence" and "for 4 days carting stone" of thirty-two shillings. Hawley died a year later and a codicil to his will set Robbin free.

A second example comes from the account book of Samuel Lyon, a well-respected landowner from Northcastle, New York, who served as a major in the Revolutionary Army and whose father, Roger Lyon, was prominent enough to have once been visited by George Washington. Lyon had a farm of about two hundred and fifty acres on which he grew wheat, rye, corn, oats, flax, buckwheat, hay, and potatoes and raised cattle, horses, pigs, and a few sheep. In an account book that covered the years 1775 to 1789, he noted that "in the first year i made 124 rods" of stone wall. In an entry dated May 1, 1787, Lyon wrote that a piece of stone wall ninety four and a half rods long was made with "Amos Roberts and Lieu" making 35 rods and "Moses and Joseph Offeggins and Wheeten" making 59 and a half rods. According to Richard Landers, a New York state historian who has done extensive research on the Lyon family, Samuel Lyon definitely kept slaves, and the fact that there is no indication in this notation that the individuals who built the wall were paid for their labors and no mention of their last names, indicates that Lyon is referring to a wall that he had his slaves build.

This wall, a reminder of a past more complex than some may care to admit, may still be standing today. Many of the walls built by the Lyon family are. You can see them if you turn off Route 22 onto Chestnut Ridge in what is now Armonk, New York. Some of these old walls have been taken apart and relaid by the homeowners who now occupy the land, but others run through the woods much as they have done for two centuries. A few are in such good stead that one might think they had been built only yesterday—except for their texture and color, a lichen-encrusted, hurricane gray and green that takes a wall a very long time to acquire.

In any portrait of the wall builders of early New England, the Yankee farmer must move over to allow room for Native Americans and black slaves. He must also share credit for this work with other laborers of the time—his children who helped haul the stone and dig the foundation of many walls, and indentured servants, a type of laborer often found in the colonies. Even as late as the nineteenth century, it was not unusual for a boy to be bound out to a farmer "to learn the art and mystery of husbandry." This was the case with Asa Sheldon, the Yankee drover, who began work at the age of six, picking stones out of a neighbor's field, and was bonded out at eleven for twenty dollars in cash and the promise of one hundred dollars when he turned twenty-one. But what Sheldon learned was not so much the lessons of farming as how unreasonable and harsh men can be. Sheldon's employer allowed him one pair of shoes every two years (in winter, Sheldon was forbidden to slide on the ice for fear that he might wear out these rare commodities more quickly) and he was permitted neither an overcoat nor boots. Sometimes, he was given so little time for meals that he had to eat his meager fare—a few ears of boiled Indian corn, for example—while hurrying out to the fields. When Sheldon wrote his autobiography many years later, he remembered those years with some bitterness and he beseeched fathers to "never be guilty of such a rash act. Never bind your children to service of any kind."

Of course, Yankee farmers also built walls. Account books make it clear that farmers built walls and hauled stone for themselves in all seasons (wall building is a task that can be done at any time of the year, excepting, of course, when it is too wet to move rocks safely or too cold to dig a foundation). Some farmers—even farmers wealthy enough to have owned slaves—also hired themselves out to build walls for those who did not have the bent for wall building or the time. The account book of Stephen Horton, the owner of a general store in Yonkers, New York, in the early 1800s contains numerous entries of payment to several different individuals for "work done at wall," "days digging stone," "drawing stone for chimney," and so on. Like most store owners and village dwellers of his day, Horton was also a part-time farmer, but perhaps because he was a store-owner, he could pay his laborers in cash. His wage to one wall builder in 1802 was one dollar a day, a good wage considering that the average daily wage for that period was only seventy-seven cents.

Wall building in the early nineteenth century was not a highly specialized trade (that would come towards the middle of the century when gangs of expert wall builders moved through the countryside erecting walls at so much a rod), but even in the eighteenth century, there were those who devoted most of their time to the craft. Asa Sheldon said that his father, for example, "owning but few acres of land, worked much of the time stoning wells and cellars, and consequently was with his family but little."

Sheldon's father may have been paid in cash for his labors, but often the men who built walls for others were paid in kind (a labor swap with one man building a wall in exchange for having his hides tanned or his shoes made) or sometimes in goods—wheat, corn, or perhaps liquor. In 1768, in the town of Portsmouth, New Hampshire, an elaborate agreement was drawn up stating the terms under which Joseph Tucker would build a wall for a merchant named Woodbury Langdon. Langdon was to provide "Oxen and all tools necessary as he usually hath done," and Tucker was to be paid "one gallon and an half of Rum for each Rod the said stone wall may measure." A rod, remember, is sixteen and a half feet; although a good man might be able to build half a rod of wall a day, if Tucker consumed much of his salary, he could hardly have matched that pace.

The tools referred to in the agreement between Langdon and Tucker would have been the few, simple tools used everywhere for building stone walls in the eighteenth century: a crowbar (a length of iron flattened at one end), a mason's hammer to knock the odd corner off a piece of rock, a pick, a spade or shovel for clearing the ground for a foundation, and a stone boat for hauling the rock. Because of their flat bottoms, stone boats moved over rough terrain and roads much better than wagons. They actually repaired roads as they were dragged along and toll roads often welcomed them while they might prohibit or charge an extra toll for wagons.

Oxen were used to pull the stone boats, and the oxen that Langdon supplied for Tucker were probably the local variety——red or red-and-white beasts distantly related to the purebred Devons that some of the first colonists had brought over from Devonshire. Today, when only a few farmers still keep oxen, all that most of us have to remind us of these once numerous creatures are the recipes for ox-tail soup that linger in such comprehensive cookbooks as the *Joy of Cooking* and a few phrases such as "dumb as an ox," "patient as an ox," and, of course, "strong as an ox." But like Indians and slaves, oxen are also unsung heros of New England's stone walls. One hundred and fifty years ago, they were as familiar as they were indispensable. They plowed the fields, hauled stumps, drew stone, drove the family to church on Sunday, and provided the meat for their dinner afterward. Their brawn was absolutely necessary to the building of New England's stone walls; without them it is doubtful that New England would look the way it does.

Oxen, rather than horses, played the leading role in shaping the colonial landscape for the simple reason that they were much better suited to settlement conditions. Both horses and oxen accompanied the first settlers from England, but most of the horses didn't even survive the trip. Those that did succumbed during the first winter when they were forced to fend for themselves with little or no shelter or food. Cattle and oxen, on the other hand, managed well. Oxen are low-maintenance, hard-working animals. They did not require grooming and could survive the winter on what they could forage for themselves, supplemented perhaps by hay, straw, and a few ears of corn. As President

Madison said in a 1837 address, "The circumstance particularly recommending him [the ox], is, that he can be supported when at work, by grass and hay; while the horse requires grain and much of it."

The ability to fend for themselves was just one of many advantages of oxen over horses. Oxen were far less susceptible to injury and diseases than horses (it is said that an ox will get one injury to a horse's ten), and they had a decided economic advantage. After putting in five to seven years of work in the fields, an ox could be fattened up and butchered, providing the family with nearly a ton of meat, or, alternatively, with a substantial profit on its initial investment in the animal.

A nineteenth-century farmer with his plow, oxen, and a helper who might have been either his son, a day laborer, or an indentured servant. In the mid-1800s, some farmers were still using oxen to plow their fields, but because farming by then was far less arduous than it had been a century earlier, many others had opted for speed and switched to horses. Notes one authority, "Oxen had helped to bring civilization to the wilderness but the resulting changes created a world with no room for the working cattle."

Oxen were also much better suited to the business of breaking new soil and clearing new ground than horses—especially the light, small horses that were first sent over. Whereas horses tended to be excitable and unable to stand still for long periods of time, oxen, with their calm temperaments and their slow, steady way of pulling, were perfect for such slow-paced tasks as stump pulling, hauling stone, mending fence, and pulling logs——the stuff of settlement life. "Yoke oxen for the plough," an early settler of the New Netherlands advised his compatriots, "in as much as in new lands full of roots, oxen go forward steadily under the plough, and horses stand still, or with a start break the harness in pieces."

With all these very tangible assets, it hardly seems possible that in a short span——the 1850s, 1860s, and 1870s——horses would come to replace oxen and replace them so thoroughly that the animals which had once been almost as numerous as people were quickly turned into historical anachronisms.

There were several reasons for the change. Fashion and speed were certainly large factors since there were few who didn't prefer trotting briskly to church in a horse and buggy to trudging along in an ox cart. But most important is that these hard-working beasts worked themselves out of a job. Oxen performed the task of clearing the landscape so well that in a few generations, the job was done and they were no longer necessary. The tasks that they had been especially good at became largely obsolete. Once the stumps were all removed and the stones blasted out and hauled away, the land could be plowed by less hardy, but faster, horses.

Speeding up the transition from ox power to horse power were the agricultural inventions of the nineteenth century: threshers, reapers, and other new machines designed to make the farmer's life easier——and designed to be pulled by horse locomotion. Cast-iron ploughs rapidly took the place of wooden ones in the mid-1800s, and their significantly lighter draft sealed the ox's fate. It wasn't long before some of New England's earliest and most industrious settlers, ones with names like Buck and Bright, Amos and Andy, Nip and Tuck, and Dave and Dan, were reduced to a memory, leaving an altered landscape and, incidentally, one way of dating the stone walls that they helped to build. Since oxen were used less and less after 1800, finding an ox shoe in association with a wall is almost a sure sign that it dates from the eighteenth or very early nineteenth century.

THE "SIGNS OF a good working oxen," wrote Asa Sheldon, in 1862, a time when the number of oxen in New England was falling precipitously, are "bright hazel eye, which denotes intellect, or a disposition to receive instruction, and a readiness to obey it; long, lean head; broad between the eyes; wide, open nostrils; horns not more than medium size at the base——these show an ox keen to pull and one that can endure the heat of day...."

One wonders what the size of an animal's horns can have to do with its ability to tolerate heat, but how can one doubt the advice of a man who once

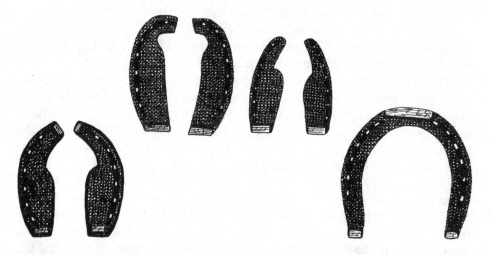

Because of the steady decline in the use of oxen in the early to mid-1800s, finding an ox shoe in association with a stone wall is an almost sure indication that the wall dates back to the early nineteenth century. Like a horse shoe, an ox shoe came in different sizes and was made from malleable iron which was forged either by hand (center two sets of shoes) or machine (horse and ox shoes at either end). But unlike a horse shoe, an ox shoe comes in two parts, one for each half of the ox's split hoof.

supervised forty oxen and their drivers in building stone culverts for the Boston and Lowell Railroad?

Sheldon also had some "hints to stone layers." To stoners of wells, he urged, "Never, on any account, lay the largest end of the stone in toward the well." And to farmers, he advised,

> Never destroy any part of the strength of your wall for the sake of making it look handsome on a farm. In reality those farm walls always look handsomest that stand best. There has been no better way found to lay farm walls than on large foundation stones, placed on cobbles. In laying a wall on low, frosty ground, where it is necessary to trench, I would recommend to fill the trench with that kind of dry gravel before mentioned for railroad trenches, walks, &c., if it can be had conveniently, or with sand if that can not be procured. Either of these are better than small stones for two reasons. First, mud will work in among small stones, freeze and heave the wall. Second, it will give more encouragement to the growth of briars and brush than gravel will.

But throughout his curiously nonreflective and impersonal autobiography (Sheldon mentions his wife only once), this New England farmer is most proud of his displays of Yankee ingenuity and of his best trades—for having the idea of putting springs on his wagon, for example, or for buying pigs in the south one year, then selling them at a huge profit in New England. Another of Sheldon's many innovations, one which involved hauling rock, underscores the virtuosity of the postcolonists when it comes to matters of stone, as well as the disappearing nature of yesterday's technology (something that believers in "precolonial contact" should keep in mind).

"I once had some stones to move that averaged about five tons each," this teamster wrote.

> I hardly knew how it could be done as wheels could not be used, the pass not being wide enough. As I stood thinking upon it for a moment, it occurred to me that good, straight, rye straw, spread crosswise of the path, would help the drag. On trying this plan I found it worked to a charm. The hotter the sun

shone, the easier the drag would slide, and I found one good yoke of oxen would slip along with five tons comfortably.

Sheldon lived in the age of improvement and was very much part and product of his time. So were the railroads and stone walls, representing as they did improved land (land unencumbered by stone) and an improved society, one in which cows were kept in their proper place—and not in the corn. Who would have believed that the old order of farming in New England was about to be turned on its head, and that, in the process, stone walls themselves would come to be seen as "encumbrances"?

8

TWO CASE STUDIES: THE LACE WALLS OF MARTHA'S VINEYARD AND SHAKER STONE WALLS

THERE is no shortage of unusual walls in New England. There are walls which make you wonder how on earth they were made and walls which leave you puzzling why they were made. There are walls which are extraordinary from a botanical point of view, those whose rocks are covered by a beautiful array of mosses or lichens; and there are those like so many in eastern Connecticut and southern Rhode Island, which are especially well constructed. There are walls which are unusually high or unusually wide and those into which unusual features——stiles, drains, creeps, deer blinds, and carriage mounts——have been built. There are those with an unusual history: the four-foot-wide, twelve-hundred-foot-long "Brother's Walk" in Hardwick, Massachusetts, built (in 1827) to connect the houses of Anson and Franklin Ruggles in order that their wives could visit without having to get their shoes wet, or the eleven-foot-high "spite wall" in Westminster, Massachusetts, which was constructed by Edmund Proctor in order to prevent his neighbor from spying on him and complaining if Proctor plowed his fields on the Sabbath. But New England's most unusual walls, I think, must be the lace walls on the island of Martha's Vineyard.

Until you have seen a lace wall, named because the stones in it have so

Two unusual features sometimes found in walls: steps and a projecting ledge or platform —these in a wall in Katonah, New York, that runs in front of a now-abandoned homesite. Though it is sometimes said that these platforms were made for holding mailboxes, it seems more likely that they served as carriage and horse mounts or as loading platforms for moving heavy objects into wagons and buckboards. They are quite common in the area around North Salem and Bedford, New York, and tend to be extremely well constructed out of very large stones.

many large spaces between them that the wall looks something like lace, you might be tempted to think you have seen everything a stone wall has to offer. Then you see one, and everything you thought you ever knew about stone walls—about how they should be built, about what makes them stable—flies out the window.

Most stone walls, whether they are double or single, are constructed so that there is as little space as possible between the stones and so that the tops lie flat—or if not flat, even. Lace walls, on the other hand, have a jagged, uneven top, and spaces the size of softballs between all the rocks. A wallbuilder on Martha's Vineyard recently described the men who built them, saying "they didn't put in a single chock rock or a single rock that wasn't needed—in fact it looks as though they left out rocks that had to be there."

These walls look like they couldn't stand through a single winter, but, in fact, they hold up very well, as long as every rock stays in place. In most stone walls, rocks stay in place largely because they rest on a level, firm platform of two or more stones. But in a lace wall, the stones are held in place as much by the weight of the stones above them as by their placement. So if you remove a rock from a lace wall, two more are likely to come tumbling down. If you remove many, the entire wall may fall. Lace walls seem to be a hastily-made, rock-miserly imitation of other walls, but they really represent an entirely new species of wall, a species with, perhaps, its own niche or function and that—however unlikely it may seem—is also successful in one important measure of a wall's success: the ability to stand for a century or two without toppling over.

NOT EVERY WALL on Martha's Vineyard is a lace wall. In the only parts of the island that were endowed with building stone—Chilmark, Gay Head, and Tisbury—there are many different types of walls. There are single walls, double walls, smooth- and rough-faced walls, cut and uncut walls, and dry and wet walls. The walls here are numerous and of so many different kinds because of the quantity of granite that the glaciers left behind; so much stone that an early report on this part of the island described it as "a wilderness of tumbled stones, looking as though Old Moshop [the central mythological character of the Algonquin Indians of Martha's Vineyard] might have dusted them out of his saltshaker some time when the earth needed a great deal of seasoning."

Those who live on Martha's Vineyard today are very proud of their walls and take an aesthetic and historical interest in them. In Chilmark, where the zoning laws contain an ordinance designed to protect them, there is also discussion of making an inventory of all the existing walls. But, despite the current interest in preserving the island's stone walls, very little is really known about these structures—about when they were built and by whom, about the reason behind the curious lace walls.

Although most people seem to assume that stone fencing came on the horizon at about the same time as English settlers—in the early 1600s—what little information historic records do contain indicates that, as in other parts of New England, stone fencing was a rather late arrival, resorted to after

A lace wall running across a hilltop in Chilmark, Massachusetts. With its airy or lacy construction—the large gaps between its stones—this wall looks extremely unstable, but according to its current owner William Eddy, it has rarely needed repairing. Many years have passed since sheep would have grazed Eddy's land, and the three Hampshires are drawn in only to make the point that Martha's Vineyard, like many of New England's offshore islands, used to be one vast sheep pasture.

common lands were divided up and timber resources had been depleted.

In a history of Martha's Vineyard, Charles E. Banks wrote that in the early colonial period, "all cattle ran at large as there were few fences. Not until 1664 was there a 'general fence' to corral their herds." As settlements grew, so did the need for fencing, and, given the island's meager supply of timber as well as its lack of building stone on all but the southwestern end, this need was met in most parts of the island by growing hedges and digging ditches. The land records of Chilmark indicate that that part of the island began to see a lot of stone fencing some time around the American Revolution and that wall building continued into the middle of the next century. The 1840s——a time when the island's whaling industry had brought about a period of great prosperity——were a boom time for wall building. During that time the walls of numerous estates and large homes were built, often by gangs of professional wall builders. By 1847, the town of Chilmark, a town of just 19.4 square miles, was estimated to have 40 miles of stone fencing. What is amazing is that Chilmark has absolutely no bedrock; all of the stone for these fences was surface rock deposited by the glaciers.

Another misconception about the stone walls of Martha's Vineyard is that they were used mainly to mark property lines and set off roadways, to serve as a place to put the rocks that were taken out of the fields. "They also may have kept a few sluggish cows in place," reads one pamphlet on the island, "but were certainly no use for confining sheep or other nimble animals."

This, as we know, is a common misconception throughout New England. People look at stone walls as they exist today, running through heavily wooded land and they assume that the land was always thus and therefore that the walls must have been erected as boundary markers. Moreover, they are unable to imagine that these walls, many of which are no more than two or three feet high, were very successful at containing animals. (Some of them, of course, were not. Historical accounts make clear that some stone walls of the postcolonial period were so sloppily built that they were not effective at confining animals even though that was their intended purpose.) What people today fail to realize is that most walls have changed since the time when they were built and utilized. Over the years, soil deposition, settling, and the loss of many stones have caused these walls to shrink considerably in height. Also, at one time, a large number of them would have been topped with rails and riders (which have long since rotted, of course) or, after 1870, a strand or two of barbed wire, turning these piles of rocks into far more effective barriers.

Many of the boulders which were left by the glaciers on the rocky parts of Martha's Vineyard were too large to be dragged out of the fields, even with the aid of teams of oxen, so the farmers and wall builders of the island became adept at blasting and splitting these rocks into smaller pieces, often producing regular slabs that could also be used as gate posts and foundation stones. The

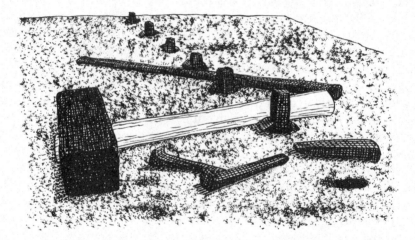

Pin and feathering came into use in the late eighteenth century and represented a substantial improvement over the existing rock-splitting techniques of ice, fire, or gun powder. It required a stone mason's hammer and a long, octagonally shaped chisel or hand drill (to drill or chisel out the holes), as well as iron pins (lower left) and feathers or wedges (lower right). Two pins were inserted into each hole with a feather between them. The feathers were then struck, one after the other, in rotation, producing split stone with a remarkably even face.

techniques they used were the same ones being used all over New England, some of which are described in the 1790 *Georgical Dictionary*.

"Stones that are very large, and which cannot with ease be removed whole, may be blown to pieces with gun powder," it notes. "They will be not only better for removing, but far better to put into walls."

The farmer's compendium goes on to mention a second method of breaking rocks, which, it says, "ought to be generally known, and which sometimes turns out cheaper." That method is to "drill two holes in a stone, ranging with the grain, when that can be discovered with the eye. Then filling each hole with two semicylindrical pieces of iron, drive a long steel wedge between them. The stone will thus be split open. And commonly, very regular shaped pieces for building may be thus obtained." This technique, also known as pin and wedging and pin and feathering (the wedge was also known as a feather), was frequently used on Martha's Vineyard, as is evident from its characteristic marks, two-to-five-inch long grooves along one of the edges of the split rock's face, which can be seen on the rocks of many of the island's walls, gateposts, and foundations.

The dictionary also mentions a third method, which is "to burn an inflammable piece of dry wood, laid on the part where you wish a rock to open. Thus the rock is heated in a straight line, and may be made to open in that part, by a smart blow of a maul. This method often answers well when the stones are flat shaped." But it fails to note a fourth that I have been told was practiced on Martha's Vineyard and elsewhere: that of drilling holes in a rock, filling those holes with water, then hoping that the expansion of the water as it freezes would split the rock. This method would probably leave traces very much like those of pin and feathering since the process of hand drilling the holes would have been the same.

As to Martha's Vineyard's wall builders, there is much more anecdote than fact. However, as already noted, it is often said that farmers frequently hired the local population of Algonquin Indians to build walls. Not too long ago, in Chilmark's town hall, three islanders were overheard having a conversation about walls and wall builders.

Jonathan Mayhew: I always heard that the Indians built them, not for

The gate posts of Chilmark's town pound showing the marks that are left by pin and feathering. These two-to-five-inch grooves or half-holes are the remains of hand-drilled holes. They are found on many of Martha's Vineyard's foundation stones and gate posts and indicate the extent of quarrying that took place on this island which, amazingly, has only surface stone and lacks any bedrock.

themselves, but for the white men who hired them.

David Flanders: All I know is that they had wooden sleds they put them on and a team of horses or oxen. They had to find some use for the stones they got out of the fields.

Chris Murphy: Hollis Smith knows all about them. I think he must have told me about crews of fishermen who'd work building the walls when the season for fishing was over. Dagget down on the north shore had a crew of men he'd hire out.

Flanders: When you look at the size of those base stones in some of the walls, you know they took at least two men and a team of oxen.

Mayhew: I heard they used four men and two yoke of oxen, one team on either side of the wall. A ditch was dug in a straight line for the base stones. They'd hitch the rock to be pulled one way or another until it settled in the right place.

Murphy: You've heard of the whiskey walls, haven't you? Well, the owner or foreman would put a bottle of whiskey a good work distance down the line. The bottle was consumed when that point was reached.

Bystander: Craig Kingsbury told me that one years ago. He said it explained why some walls were less straight than others.

And apparently whiskey was not the only drug used by wall builders. In the process of rebuilding old walls, several modern-day wall builders have turned up old medicine bottles that still bear labels indicating that they had once contained coca leaves. This is not surprising since in the late 1800s cocaine was widely available in many different recreational and medicinal forms and was commonly used to treat everything from asthma and catarrh to hunger and thirst. But wall builders may have been particularly prone to experimenting with cocaine-containing mixtures because of the enervating nature of their work. A 1912 advertisement for a twenty-five-cent box of Coca-Bola, "a masticating or chewing paste made from the leaves of the Peruvian cocoa plant," stated that "a small portion chewed occasionally acts as a powerful tonic to the muscular and nervous system, relieving fatigue and exhaustion, and enabling the user to perform additional mental and physical labor without evil after-effects."

OF ALL THE conundrums posed by the walls of Martha's Vineyard, the lace walls are still the most puzzling. There are a number of theories as to why they were built the way they were but, as far as I know, no proof for any of them. Some believe that the people who built the lace walls built them with holes because they were short on rocks and wanted to make what they had go as far as it could. Others believe that the walls were laid by people who were paid for every foot of wall they constructed. Neither of these theories can be taken very seriously. The fields near the lace walls still contain many large boulders;

A Galloway dyke on a moor in the southwest of Scotland. Though the upper tiers of this wall may seem carelessly built (as do Martha's Vineyard's lace walls), each of the stones rests on at least three bearings and has, in fact, been carefully placed to allow the light to show through. Sheep, not even the black-faced sheep pictured here, will attempt such a wall, but even in Scotland this advantage is not widely understood. In the years since dykes such as these were constructed, many of them have had their holes filled in by well-meaning individuals.

moreover, any farmer who contracted a jobber to build a normal wall would hardly be satisfied with this see-through and seemingly insubstantial alternative.

A more plausible theory, and one that is widely circulated, is that lace walls were built so as to allow the wind to blow through them rather than against them. Not too long ago, when Martha's Vineyard was a treeless place, it was also very windy, and wind can topple walls (one description of a violent storm in New York in 1797 remarked that the winds were of such force that "heavy stonewalls were swept level with the ground, and large stones of 300 pounds weight moved to a considerable distance"). Substantiating this theory is the fact that lace walls do tend to be found on hilltops and running in an east-west direction, counter to the prevailing winds.

But, however good this theory is, it doesn't take into account that in Scotland, there is a kind of wall very much like the lace walls of Martha's Vineyard and that this wall, called a Galloway dyke, was built with two specific purposes in mind: to deal with a wide variety of stone (such as the glacial debris covering Martha's Vineyard) and to deter black-faced sheep, already mentioned as one of the sheep types of the colonial era.

Galloway dykes, known in Scotland from the early 1700s, differ somewhat from the lace walls of Martha's Vineyard in that their bases—their lower halves—were usually double walls which were then topped by twenty-two inches or so of single, widely spaced stones that allowed the light to shine through. But listen to what an author in the early eighteenth century had to say about them: "These walls have such a tottering and alarming appearance that all kinds of stock are terrified to attempt them, and as an additional recommendation they require fewer stones and are more expeditiously built and last as long as double stone walls without lime."

Colonel F. Rainsford-Hannay, whose book *Dry Stone Walling* is the authoritative text in England, says that the Galloway dyke is a "highly effective" deterrent to an adventurous ewe, and he recommends that when studying one of these walls, one "ought to stoop down to the height of a sheep. From that height, 18 inches above ground level, the dyke looks most formidable. . . ." Following his advice, I crouched down in front of a lace wall on Martha's

Vineyard. With the light shining through it, the wall did indeed look as if it might fall at any moment.

As to whether there were farmers on the island who would have known about the advantages of this unusual type of construction, Martha's Vineyard never saw any large-scale immigration from Scotland, but there were a few Scotsmen on the island from as early as the 1600s, including one of the earliest immigrants to the island, the builder of the Scotsman's Bridge on State Road that is still in existence. The town records also reveal a sprinkling of Scotsmen living in Chilmark in the 1800s.

So here's another theory to explain the riddle of Martha's Vineyard's lace walls. I wish I could say that it was more than just a theory, but historical records—like the lace walls themselves—are full of holes and the largest ones seem to be where the records of agriculture and farm practices should go.

This massive, granite block wall contains pieces of granite up to a yard across. It dates back to 1793, just one year after the Shaker Community at Canterbury, New Hampshire, was formed, and it is possible that its stones were left over from quarrying the foundation stones for the first Canterbury buildings. The low, sideless wheelbarrow in front of the wall is called a stone barrow; it was useful for moving smaller stones that did not require oxen and a stone boat.

WHEN TIMOTHY DWIGHT, the Yale University president who is best remembed for his journals on eighteenth-century American life, passed through a Shaker village in 1799, he wrote that, "everything about them was clean and tidy.... Even their stables, the fences which surround their fields, and the road which passes through their village are all uncommonly neat." Shakers, at the time, had only been in this country for twenty-five years (the eight original Shakers had sailed from Liverpool in 1774); yet, despite impoverished beginnings, they already had a reputation for simplicity, orderliness, and economy, a reputation that would endure until the present when just a few Shakers remain.

Founded on the principles of celibacy and consecrated labor, the Shakers were led by Ann Lees whose beliefs and religious fervor were very influenced by a deprived childhood and the death of her four children in infancy (for which she came to blame her previous sexual appetite). Scarred by these early experiences, Lees sought to bring heaven to earth by creating a perfect and orderly society; she and her followers succeeded in establishing the most successful utopian community this country has ever known. By 1840, the number of Shakers had grown from eight to 6,000 and the number of Shaker communities to eighteen.

As with most other American religious associations of the eighteenth and nineteenth centuries, the Shakers built their spiritual foundations on good tillage. When Lees led her small group to the New World, land in remote places could still be had for very little and farming was the logical means of subsistence. But farming to the Shakers was not just a means for survival; rather, cultivation of the fields was part of their larger scheme to deliver the world from its evils. The Shakers believed that only by using land to the maximum did they acknowledge God's blessings. They also believed that physical labor promoted both spiritual and temporal values; it was good for the mind, the soul, and the collective welfare. It had the benefits of mortifying lust, teaching humility, creating order and convenience, supplying a surplus for charity, and supporting and insulating the fraternity.

In many ways, the actual husbandry practiced by the Shakers was very similiar to that of the more conscientious subsistence farmers of the same era.

Brother Nehemiah White (1823-87) and eleven Shaker boys under his supervision during a break from their labors in the fields of the Canterbury community. If these boys were typical of the children brought up by the Shakers, notes Priscilla Brewer, author of *Shaker Communities, Shaker Lives,* perhaps only one of the eleven would actually join the Society upon reaching adulthood.

But in one important way it was different, giving groups of Shakers a huge advantage over the individual farmer. Since Shaker husbandry was based on a large labor pool, the believers, as they were called, were able to quickly turn raw, uncleared land and forests into well-ordered fields and well-filled barns. The picture of prosperity they created must have been responsible for many conversions, and the Shakers, it is said, were not above proselytizing on the grounds of economic benefit.

The advantages of this labor pool extended to the community's fences. Whereas an individual yeoman would have begun fencing his land with stumps, then rail fences, and only getting around to building stone walls after decades or generations of farming, at the Shaker Community in Canterbury, New Hampshire, the Shakers fenced early and—with the exception of a few picket fences—only in stone. The community was founded in 1792, and at least one of its walls dates back to almost that same year. This is an extraordinary wall, incorporating as it does huge blocks of granite, several of which measure more than a yard in length and width and must each weigh, therefore, 4,000 pounds or more. (A cubic foot of granite weighs about 150 pounds.) A wall with stones this size does not move about and will require little or no maintenance over the years. This one stands today very much as it must have two hundred years ago, a testimony to the people who built it and to their belief that they should make things as if they would die tomorrow but the thing must last a thousand years.

Located as it is in the state which has come to be known as "the Granite State," the community at Canterbury, one of only two communities that are still inhabited by living Shakers, may have been better endowed with building stone than any other Shaker community. Historians have suggested, in fact, that the rockiness of Canterbury's land was responsible for the pursuit there of an economy based more on manufacturing, cloth making, and stock raising than on agriculture. Be that as it may, every field and orchard in the 6,000 acres that used to belong to the Canterbury Shakers (over the years they have sold off parcels and now own only 600 acres) is surrounded by a stone wall.

What is interesting is that the walls are of so many different types. If you approach the village from the south, the first wall that you come to is the one with the enormous granite blocks, but not two hundred feet from this wall are some four other distinct wall types. There is a low wall made of long, somewhat narrow slabs of granite that had been cut out of larger pieces of rock (using the pin-and-feathering technique) and a very wide wall made out of field stones. There is a wall with capping stones and one with drainage holes, and walls which have a smooth face on one side but not the other. Then there is a wall made entirely of small field stones weighing no more than perhaps fifteen pounds each——one-man stones, a stone mason would call them, because one man could easily pick them up.

My husband and I puzzled over this last wall and its small stones and finally decided that it had probably been built with stones picked out of fields that had been cultivated for potatoes or some other root crop. We were wrong, I found out, when I spoke to Eldress Bertha Lindsey, Canterbury's last remaining leader——and the only living Shaker leader anywhere——and asked her about this particular wall. The wall had been built, she said, by a one-armed man in the early 1800s. The stones are small because he couldn't handle bigger ones, Bertha explained, adding that "he must have been very dedicated to what he was doing."

The historical records of Canterbury——the journals and diaries of the Shakers who lived there——contain some brief references to wall building, but no lengthy discourses on the techniques of wall building and sketchy indication as to when most of the walls were built. But according to Eldress Bertha, who was placed at Canterbury in 1905 as a seven-year-old orphan and who has been a member of the Society since 1918, when at twenty-one years of age she was allowed to join, "they must have gotten done with that particular task by the late 1800s because nothing like that was being done when I came here." Some of the wall builders were probably men who had learned their skill before joining the Shakers, but much of the labor for "this particular task," as for many of the Shaker's heaviest jobs, came from a surprising quarter——young boys: the children of converts as well as orphans the Shakers took in and children indentured to the Shakers by their parents or guardians. Shaker leaders felt that the best Shakers were made young, and in the early 1800s, they were only too glad to accept a large number of indentured children. Soon, however, they found that this method of increasing their membership often backfired, resulting in long and bitter court battles. As Priscilla Brewer, author of *Shaker Communities, Shaker Lives*, points out, "Worldly parents of this period discovered that they could leave their children with the Shakers for brief periods while they re-established themselves after economic or geographic dislocation. Even if they signed indentures, they knew that sympathetic Worldly judges were likely to decide custody cases in their favor."

In a Shaker community, boys and girls were separated and lived in special quarters under the supervision of several adults. The male Shakers responsible for the boys usually kept a journal of their activities, and from these records we know that the boys went to school from November to March, but did farm work——planting, harvesting, cutting wood, hauling stone, building fence—— the rest of the year. An entry for June 1845 from a *Boy's Journal of Work* states that "the boys have hoed the corn over once picked up stone put up fence and a great variety of other work." August, it was noted, was spent cutting fifteen acres of oats, cutting thistles, cutting adlers, digging around stone for blasting, and making fence; and September, hauling and spreading manure, making fence, and picking stone.

The lives of the boys were not all unremitting toil; the journals also record the occasional swimming and fishing trips. However, a miscellaneous item from one of these journals serves to show the extent of their labors. This item noted that in 1842, "the boys," nineteen of them in all, were responsible for planting, hoeing, and digging sixteen acres of potatoes yielding 2,400 bushels, one acre of beets yielding 850 bushels, 9 acres of corn yielding 300 bushels, as well as for raising bush beans and 1,100 pumpkins. The ages of the boys who accomplished all this were not recorded, but their heights and weights were, and they make it clear that these boys, the backbone of the Shaker labor force, could not have been very old. These nineteen boys ranged in height from just three feet six inches (the height of today's slightly less-than-average three year old) to five feet two and a half inches and in weight from 38 pounds to 113 pounds. The Shakers took orphans in as a charity, but it is obvious that they stood to gain a great deal: a ready and cheap labor force and, what is equally important in a celibate society, potential converts. But converts they did not

One of several, solid granite stoops carved by hand by Brother Macajah Tucker of the Shaker community in Canterbury. This stoop has just four steps but it is also impressive. After more than one hundred years in use, the only signs of wear and tear are at the corners of the steps, around the holes that were drilled for the railings. Water was undoubtedly the culprit here; it got into these holes and froze, thereby cracking the stone around them.

often get; when most of the orphans and indentured children were old enough to join the Society, they chose instead to leave.

Despite the usefulness of the boys, the task of overseeing them was one of the least favorite of the Shakers, inspiring much grumbling, sometimes in poetic form, sometimes very humorous, from people who are often pictured as humorless and uncomplaining. An 1844 entry from a *Boy's Journal Of Work* contains this poem:

> I'm now released from the boys
> And from a deal of din + noise
> And John is left to rule the roost
> Without a second mate to boost
> My Elders gave me a good name
> So I do leave devoid of shame
> Ha Ha He He how glad I be
> I've no more boys to trouble me.
>
> But John poor John I pity him
> He's got so many sprouts to trim
> I feel his soul will be out tir'd
> In doing that he ne'r desir'd.
> O may he have a real gift
> the good from evil all to sift——
> And may I no more mind the boys
> Be troubled with their chatt'ring noise....

What the boys did not do were the jobs requiring skilled labor. They may have been the force behind many of the walls at Canterbury (and elsewhere) but they do not seem to have been involved with the simple but very fine stone work there. The granite the glaciers left behind was used to make stone walls at Canterbury, as well as numerous other objects which in less stony areas or in the hands of a less industrious people might have been made out of wood. These include gate posts, door frames, barn columns, steps, and a granite walkway a mile long. If these things had been made out of wood, as the Shakers well knew, most of them would have rotted long ago; as it is, they exist today in much the same state in which they were made over a hundred years ago. The granite walkway, made of large, square slabs of granite which were split off large boulders, chiseled to the right size, numbered, dragged out of the woods, and laid in order, has been keeping Shaker shoes dry and mud-free ever since it was made in 1834.

If anything, these other stone objects are even more impressive than the walls. My husband gasped when he saw that the five-step stoop on one of the frame buildings had been carved out of a single piece of stone. Later, I asked Eldress Bertha about those steps, and she knew immediately which ones I was referring to. They had been made, she said, by the Shaker brother Macajah Tucker, the same man who had made the granite walkway. Tucker, who had joined the Shakers as a young man in the late eighteenth century, "believed in doing perfect work." He had had some training in stone masonry before coming to the Shakers and was a highly skilled woodworker as well. According to Eldress Bertha, he used to go off into the woods to look for a piece of stone, then chisel out by hand the shape that he wanted. In one case, this was the five steps; in another, the beautifully rounded gate posts, or the long, rectangular slabs that were used as door frames.

As I spoke with her over the phone, Eldress Bertha took me on a verbal tour of the walls of Canterbury and of the work of Macajah Tucker, pointing out which steps and posts were his (the smoothest ones) and speaking in such detail that I had the impression that as we spoke, she was looking out of a second-story window at the things she was describing. It came as a great surprise, then, when she said that she was blind and had been for thirty years. She had not seen these objects and walls for all that time and yet she was describing them, referring to them as if she was looking at them that very moment. Macajah Tucker and the one-armed wall builder may have believed in perfect work, but they also lived in a community where such work was likely to be acknowledged and appreciated.

9

THE IRONY OF WALLS

Something there is that doesn't love a wall,
That sends the frozen-ground-swell under it,
And spills the upper boulders in the sun;
And makes gaps even two can pass abreast....

So begins one of Robert Frost's most famous poems, "Mending Wall."
It ends with Frost's neighbor, with whom Frost has met, "to walk the line/And
set the wall between us once again," saying as he has said already once before
in the poem, "Good fences make good neighbors."

I wish I had a nickel for every time this sentiment was taken to be the
message of this beautiful but really very subversive poem. Perhaps, per-
versely, I would take all my coins and build the stone wall of my dreams. But
"good fences make good neighbors" is not the sentiment of Frost, only of his
neighbor. Frost, on the other hand, wonders wryly, "Why do they make good
neighbors? Isn't it/ Where there are cows? But here there are no cows...." And
he says, "Before I built a wall I'd ask to know/ What I was walling in or walling
out,..."

Frost's neighbor is intent upon keeping up the New England farmer's ritual of mending fences in the spring, but "Spring is the mischief" in Frost, and he doubts the need for this task where, "He is all pine and I am apple orchard" and "My apple trees will never get across/And eat the cones under his pines...."

IF YOU DRIVE to Derry, New Hampshire, a town where roads and even motor inns are named for this well-known poet, and head to the farm where he lived and raised chickens (not successfully) from 1900 to 1911, you can still see the subject of "Mending Wall." The wall, such as it is, that divided Napoleon Guay's pine trees and Robert Frost's apple orchard is stop number fifteen on a "poetry trail" that the New Hampshire Division of Parks and Recreation has created on the land that was once Frost's Derry farm (the name itself mocks the idea that a farm can be a farm without any cows), land that has since served as an auto graveyard. Contrived as the trail may be——other stops on it include the "farm pond" where visitors are asked if they have ever tried to "find the inspiration for a poem" of their own——I was happy to be led to that exact boundary and to see that exact wall. As it stands today, it is no more than two feet high. Its stones cannot be said to have been laid; they are, rather, perched precariously, one on top of another. Now it's possible that this wall has changed dramatically since Frost's time——it may have been dismantled for some reason or the stones stolen. Then again, perhaps this poor excuse of a wall was enough to have inspired the poet. And the pitiful nature of this wall only underscores Frost's point. What was the reason for maintaining a wall——especially such an unwalllike wall——where there were no animals to keep out and no crops to keep them out of?

Frost wasn't alone in questioning this tradition; and his land——once the site of a thriving New Hampshire farm——wasn't alone in having neither crops nor livestock. "Mending Wall" only hints at the changes that were taking place in New England; but in 1913, when the poem was written, agriculture was in turmoil in New Hampshire——and throughout New England——and had been for many years. In 1860, there were 31,000 farms in New Hampshire; by 1930, there would be half that many. In many parts of New England, the trend was the same: struck by "Western fever" and unable to make their small fields profitable, farmers left their rocky plots for more fertile ground. Or they were lured away by the promise of a steady job in one of the many factories that sprang out of the industrialization of New England. Some tried to hold on to their land by taking second jobs as hatters or shoemakers, or by joining a gang of wall builders and relaying crude farm walls to suit the tastes of an increasingly affluent population (the burgeoning tourist trade that saved many areas from economic disaster). But for many this was only a temporary stopgap, the first turn in a downward spiral leading away from the family farm.

The first farms to be abandoned were the hill farms, farms carved out of the stony highlands of the Green Mountains, the White Mountains, and the Appalachians, farms where the growing season was the shortest and the air the coldest. In the early 1800s, a proliferation of roads, canals, and turnpikes

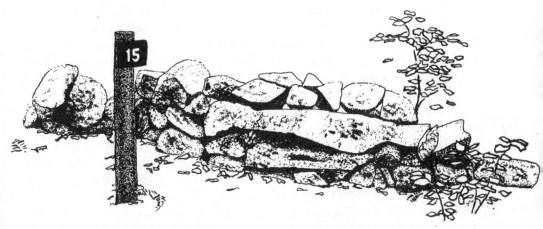

The inspiration for Robert Frost's poem "Mending Wall" is now stop number fifteen on a Parks and Recreation Poetry Trail.

brought isolated hill farmers into contact with the outside world, and with that contact, came news of western lands of "unsurpassed fertility." The exodus west began in 1825 when the Erie Canal was opened; it reached epidemic proportions in the 1850s and continued for several decades after. In Vermont where one-half of the native-born Vermonters had left the state by 1850, entire towns picked up and moved. What they left behind reverted to wilderness.

"Some of those mountain townships present an aspect of singular abandonment," Herman Melville wrote after visiting northern New England in the 1850s. "Though they have never known aught but peace and health, they, in one lesser aspect at least, look like countries depopulated by plague and war. Every mile or two a house is passed untenanted." Today, parts of the Appalachian Trail lead down the main streets of some of these once-substantial towns—New England's ghost towns. All that is left to mark their former existence are cellar holes and miles of stone walls.

While the growth of industry and manufacturing in New England should have continued to be a boon to the region's farmers, it proved instead to be another drain, especially on the hilltop communities and other areas of small, marginal farms. Here at last was the home market New England's farmers needed to make their farms into something more than self-subsistent enterprises; but beginning in the 1840s and 1850s, farmers had to compete for this market with cheap produce that was coming in by rail from the western states of Ohio, Indiana, and Illinois.

Western farmers had significant advantages of size, scale, and fertile soil. If eastern farmers were to stay in business, it was clear that they too would have to farm on a large scale. But farming on a large scale meant using such new, horse-powered machinery as the McCormick reaper, horse rakes, and seed drills, and the very great irony of the stone walls of New England is that they helped to make the use of these fast but often cumbersome machines impossible. In the small fields that many New England farmers had so laboriously created, it was difficult to turn around with anything larger than an ox-drawn plow. So in all but a few areas of New England (the Connecticut Valley, for example), use of the new machines (some of which were designed to be pulled by several teams of horses) was out of the question. Farmers now had their market, but they could supply it only at great cost: either they abandoned their traditions and began the backbreaking process of dismantling their walls and combining their fields or they abandoned their land and started over elsewhere.

Notes John Stilgoe, author of *The Common Landscape of America, 1580-1845*, "Mass-produced farm machinery dramatically reshaped the size and topography of fields wherever farmers could afford to purchase the latest inventions. ... Machinery was designed for typical fields, and progressive farmers quickly discovered that such fields were those of Pennsylvania and the new western states: large, flat, and rock-free."

This crisis in New England, though unanticipated, was actually a long time in the making. New England farmers, as we know, had divided up their land and fenced their fields under the assumption that "small fields produce best"; "in conformity with the accepted view," as Clarence Danhof, an authority on American fencing practices, observes, "that an abundance of adequate fences was an indispensable adjunct to good and successful farming." The earliest European settlers of the area had come to perceive fencing as an unconditional good—a perception that arose out of their critical, chronic need for fences coupled with the great local abundance of fencing materials—and this perception was passed down through the generations and gradually translated into tradition. In the beginning, of course, small lots made sense. When the first colonists were clearing the land and gradually fencing it, in wood, then in stone, much of the work of clearing, planting, plowing, and harvesting had to be done by hand and small fields were all that most families could manage.

"Men understood the great effort required to clear fields larger than one or two acres," Stilgoe also points out, "and slowly—especially in New England—they learned how much longer they spent clearing one eight-acre field than eight one-acre ones."

As time went on, though, the fencing traditions of New England, together with the country's fencing laws, had evolved into an increasingly unmanageable, uneconomic situation. Fencing laws only required the protection of crops, but fencing traditions encouraged dividing up arable land into small fields. Then, to make matters worse, as improved breeding practices were adopted in the early eighteenth century, even more enclosures were called for. Farmers were advised to separate their animals by dividing up and fencing their pasture land into discrete fields. This had definite advantages ("Cattle when turned into a pasture are uneasy—they will roam over the whole pasture, cropping here a little and there a little—treading and wasting as much as they can eat," a farmer wrote in a letter to *The Farmer's Monthly Visitor* in 1852. "In a small lot they get over their roaming sooner, and go to eating in earnest."), but farmers now had a double dose of fencing to erect and maintain: fences to stop animals from breeding at random with each other and fences to protect crops from animals.

Although fences of the latter type—those required by fencing laws— made sense during the early days of a settlement, by the mid-1800s in most parts of New England, they had lost their economic rationale. By then, many areas were so settled, cleared, and farmed that the cost of fencing animals out of tillable fields exceeded that of fencing them within their own pastures. The existence of mature settlements called for fence legislation which would make animal owners wholly responsible for controlling their livestock, but courts, legislatures, and farmers were all slow to recognize that the change from frontier to mature settlement had taken place.

Fencing laws and fencing traditions translated into a huge burden for farmers. In the 1850s and 1860s, the cost of fencing a farm in New England often exceeded the selling value of the farm. In New York, in 1860, the amount of capital invested in fencing averaged out to $900 per farm or a total of $67 million. In the same year, the value of all of Maine's fences was $25 million and of New Jersey's, $21 million. In 1871, the United States Department of Agriculture valued the investment of the entire nation in fencing at $1.75 billion. By contrast, the value of all livestock, as reported in the 1860 census, was $1.089 billion and the value of all farms, $6.645 billion. The onus of fencing was felt everywhere, but in the West, where there was a lack of every kind of fencing material, it acquired the dimensions of a scourge. In 1830, the *Western Agriculturist* called it "the leak which prevents the filling up of our cup of bliss . . . the fretting leprosy of the land."

"We cannot do without some fencing in America," the *American Agricul-*

turist, a leading advocate of fencing reform argued in 1845. ''But to be forced to build innumerable lines of it in every direction is a positive curse to the country, and a plague upon its morality and industry. It would be hardly possible for law or custom, in a free community, to invent and put in practice anything more burdensome, unjust, and tyrannical upon the agricultural class, than the present system of fencing.''

And in 1848, commenting on the stone walls of New England, that publication asked, ''how many thousands of miles of stone wall are made for no other purpose than to get rid of the stones, without adding at all to the utility

Harvesting oats with a horse-drawn harvester on a western farm. The nineteenth century saw a revolution in farm machinery but it was a revolution which would signal the end for many Yankee farmers. The new machinery, designed to be used on the wide-open fields of western Pennsylvania, Ohio, and Illinois, was not at all suited to the small, walled fields of most New England farms.

or ornament of the farm? I venture to say, that at least one-half of the whole extent of the stone walls of New England might be advantageously dispensed with; or, by making the boundary and road fences of heavier and more durable character, fewer subdivisions would be required, and the enclosures all the better for profitable cultivation."

In other issues of the publication, stone walls, once the pride of farmers and a measure of their competence and success, were presented in a new and sinister light. They were accused of hindering the New England farmer's ability to compete and said to "disfigure" the land, to be "an eyesore in the landscape."

For most New Englanders, this connection between small, walled fields and the competitiveness of their farms must have been a difficult one to face. At the same time that the *American Agriculturist* was carrying on its campaign for reform, other journals continued to support the old traditions of small fields and divided pastures. In the same period, then, one could read that fences "contribute much to the good appearance of the farm" (in *The Cultivator*) or that they "totally mar the beauty of the landscape" (in the *American Agriculturist*). One could read that "good fences prevent eructations of bile among neighbors..." or that they are "the occasion of more angry words and brutal personal conflicts, sometimes ending with the death of one or both of the parties to it, law suits, and lasting ill-feelings among neighbors, than all other causes put together." In the 1840s and 1850s, the population was divided on the subject of fencing, with the majority continuing to believe in the old traditions and a minority calling for reform of both fencing laws and fencing customs to bring them in line with the specific fencing needs of each region of the country.

But to blame fencing and small fields for all of New England's agricultural and economic difficulties was certainly to misplace much responsibility that should have gone to the land itself, land, that as one observer has said, would still be largely given up to forests "had the Puritans gone up the Mississippi and settled on the rich lowlands of the Middle States." The small, walled fields of New England's farms may have put some farmers out of business, but in most cases they had only hastened the inevitable; the hilly, rocky, exhausted soil of their farms would never have been a match against those of the western states.

In fact, many of those New England farmers who did have low-lying farms, farms with good fertile soil, were able to survive the tumultuous decades of the mid-nineteenth century. But in order to do so, they had to quickly adapt their output to take into account competition from the West. Farmers in the West could produce wheat, sheep, and fat cattle far more cheaply than could those in the East, so it was necessary for them to get out of those operations and into something that could make them money. Some turned to tobacco, orchards, and market gardens, but most took a calculating look at the milk-hungry populations of the large cities and industrial mill towns and dedicated themselves to dairying. By the 1860s, hay was New England's leading farm crop, and milk, butter, and cheese were its chief sources of income. And despite a steady decline in the number of farms, the area's agricultural output actually increased.

On many of these surviving farms, farmers also found it necessary to dismantle many of the walls that divided and subdivided their fields. Sometimes the stone was sold for use in building, but other times the walls were simply buried in a deep trench running parallel to the length of the wall. The farmer who went to the trouble of burying a wall often followed the advice of some later agricultural writers and turned that wall into a stone drain, what was also known as a farmer's drain or, sometimes, a poor man's drain because it was a less expensive (and less effective) alternative to drains made of tile.

"Of course, the reason for building fences such as this [extensive stone walls] is that there are stones to be cleared from the land," noted George Waring in the 1877 edition of his *Book of the Farm*,

> but it would be much cheaper to bury the larger stones where they lie, by digging pits under them and dropping them out of reach of the plow, while the smaller ones could be disposed of much more cheaply, and in a way to do good instead of harm, by digging large trenches and making stone drains. It costs less to dig a ditch four feet deep and two feet wide, on an average, and put the stone in them than to lay up a good wall of the same

dimensions. In the one case we make a serviceable drain, and in the other we encumber the land and obstruct cultivation.

Nobody knows how many walls were disposed of in this way, how many miles of stone fencing in New England and New York runs three feet or so below the ground. Developers have told me that they have come across these stone drains while doing soil tests on land that was once farmland. And if you walk through the woods, in areas that have not been developed since they were abandoned as farm land, you get some idea of the density of stone wall that was once everywhere in New England, and conversely, an idea of how much stone wall must have been taken down in those areas where development and reutilization of the land *has* taken place. Also, there are those who remember well the laborious task of burying walls and they say that it was once a common practice.

Drew Outhouse, whose family has owned and operated the Outhouse Orchards in North Salem, New York, since the early 1900s, spent much of his youth burying stone walls. It was a job that——like the land——had been in the family for a while. Drew's father had also put in long days at this back-breaking task, but his stint at wall burying had occurred before the Outhouses had acquired a bulldozer to do the hardest part of the job——digging the trench, the part that Drew's father hated the most.

When the Outhouses bought their land, it——like most of the land in the area——was crisscrossed with walls, carved up into innumerable fields no larger than a couple of acres each. "This didn't make sense for an orchard," says Drew Outhouse today. "My grandfather wanted to plant long rows of apple trees and he wanted to be able to tend his trees without having to move through a lot of different fields and gateways." So the walls had to come down. Sometimes the family was able to sell the field stone to builders and masons who then carted it away, but usually the walls——or stone-wall fences as the Outhouses called them——were turned into drains.

To make these drains, first a trench was dug five to six feet deep. At the bottom of this trench, two rows of flat stones were laid. Then these two rows were capped with another, single row of flat stones, thereby forming a passageway for water. The drains were finished off by filling in the trenches with small stones, then with hay and at least two feet of earth. "In wet weather," notes Mr. Outhouse, a tall, hefty man in his forties who is now the superintendent of transportation in North Salem, "you can still hear the water running through them."

Not all of the rocks in a wall could be used to make these drains. The large foundation stones were often too big to be moved and had to be blown up instead. This, says Mr. Outhouse, was his grandfather's job, one that he approached with considerable relish and an unlimited supply of dynamite (obtained in exchange for storage space he gave to the Hercules Powder Company). Family legend has it that Drew's grandfather used to spend all day at this business of blowing up stones. "He would put one pile of sticks beneath a rock," his grandson reminisces. "Then as soon as those had gone off, he'd rush in with another stick to finish off the job."

This might seem a somewhat cavalier, light-hearted approach to disposing of these monuments of human effort, but the Outhouses had not built any of the walls they were doing away with. If they had, they might not have been so ready with their dynamite. They, like many other farmers in New York and New England, might have felt tied by these objects——the stuff of their own sweat and blood——to old, outdated methods. For this is certainly another, terrible irony of these walls, that farmers had no sooner replaced their perishable wooden fences with stone ones than those very objects prevented them from adapting to the new conditions created by the advent of farm machinery and large-scale farming practices. If the Outhouses were spared this, it was, perhaps, because the walls that they and their ancestors had actually built (along with the land that their family had farmed for two hundred years) were under water, a small part of New York City's newly constructed reservoir system. In the early 1900s, the Outhouses had been forced to sell their land to the city and start over elsewhere; that move, however difficult, may have actually been a boon.

There are other ironies to New England's stone walls. One is that the marginal, largely self-subsistent farmers of New England no sooner had a home market and were gearing up to supply it than they lost most of that market to western competition. Another is that the stone walls of New England, those fixed boundaries whose ancestors (of brush and rails) had once meant the end of the Indian way of life, contributed finally to the end for many of those who had replaced that way of life with their own. Once in place, stone walls became a conservative force, a very weighty reason to believe in tradition. By the 1860s, many of them stood as staunch and lone guardians of that belief while the fields they enclosed turned from pasture into scrub and then forest.

"I farm a pasture where the boulders lie/As touching as a basketful of eggs," Frost also wrote in a poem entitled "Of the Stones of the Place" in which an old Yankee farmer speaks to a grandson who has left for the West.

> And though they're nothing anybody begs,
> I wonder if it wouldn't signify
>
> For me to send you one out where you live
> In wind-soil to a depth of thirty feet,
> And every acre good enough to eat,
> As fine as flour put through a baker's sieve.
>
> I'd ship a smooth one you could slap and chafe,
> And set up like a statue in your yard,
> An eolith palladium to guard
> The West and keep the old tradition safe.
>
> Carve nothing on it. You can simply say
> In self-defense to quizzical inquiry:
> "The protrait of the soul of my Gransir Ira.
> It came from where he came from anyway."

PART IV

THE WALLS OF AFFLUENCE

10

WALLS OF AFFLUENCE

WHEN Irene Zegarelli drives through Tarrytown, New York, a village in Westchester County located about twenty-five miles north of New York City, she is always looking to the right and to the left——not at the houses and buildings——but at the walls that line the roads, many of which were built by her father, Giacomo Ceconi, an immigrant from northern Italy at the turn of the century. "For me it's very nostalgic," says Mrs. Zegarelli, a petite woman in her sixties with lively brown eyes and a warm, infectious laugh. "When I go around the village and touch the stones that I know my father laid, I feel very proud. I'm touching him again."

Mrs. Zegarelli's father came to the United States and to Westchester County in 1906, at the age of twenty when, after having been apprenticed to a stone cutter in Germany for six years, he, like so many skilled workers in his country, was unable to find work. Here, on the other hand, his particular skills were much in demand. America was in the throes of industrialization, and laborers were needed to build railroads, factories, offices, and everything else that accompanied this country's new-found affluence. Since the 1840s, wealthier urban dwellers, eager to flee the dirt, disease, and fire hazards of the cities, had been building houses within commuting distance of their city offices. Tarrytown and its environs became home to the country estates of the Goulds and Rockefellers, as well as many other notable New Yorkers, and stone masons such as Giacomo Ceconi were kept very busy laying walls and building bridges.

Ceconi, who died in 1973, is perhaps best remembered as the carver of the beautiful Fremont Bowl and Fountain on Broadway in Tarrytown, but he also did most of the intricate stonework on the Union Church of Pocantico (which houses the once-controversial stained-glass windows by Matisse and Chagall) and on the entrance gates of the Sleepy Hollow Cemetery. One of his greatest accomplishments was the walls of the Japanese gardens on the Rockefeller estate, walls in which the stones have been cut "pencil thin" in order to give the desired delicate effect. Ceconi's daughter regrets that her father didn't keep a record of all the projects he had worked on, but, she says, he would never have considered doing such a thing. "He was so modest that he wouldn't even take credit for the Fremont Bowl—because someone else had helped to lay two of the stones at the top," Mrs. Zegarelli remembers. "I would say, 'Oh, Papa, forget about those two stones. Don't you know that Michelangelo had students who helped him?'"

In Tarrytown, Ceconi's mark—the mark of a talented and imaginative stone cutter—is not only to be found in the provinces of the wealthy. Ceconi, like many other Italian stone masons, also made walls for himself and his neighbors. And Tarrytown, like other towns where large numbers of Italian immigrants concentrated (Croton-on-Hudson is another), is filled with examples of this somewhat less grand, but skilled and unusual stone work. In North Tarrytown, Ceconi owned different houses at different times and he and his sons (two of whom went into bricklaying) built stone walls around each. They are all handsome; they are all different, as if Ceconi was using his own property as a sketch pad on which to experiment with different styles and ideas. Some of them are very natural looking walls of uncut field stones; others are more formal, sometimes with unusual features, such as planters for flowers, built into them.

"I don't think people realize just how much goes into stonework, that it doesn't just happen," Mrs. Zegarelli told me as we walked around looking at these different walls. "I tried to make a rock garden once, but it didn't turn out very well. You have to know what you're doing—where to put a big stone, how to achieve just the right balance and proportion."

"I used to enjoy talking to my father about aesthetics, about proportion and balance," she said later. "Though because he was so modest and quiet, sometimes it was like pulling teeth. My father would pick up a stone and he'd say, 'There's the heart of the stone. There's its meat and its veins.' Then he would start chiseling and before long he would be left with something beautiful—a stone with interesting color and texture."

THOUGH THE LATE nineteenth and early twentieth centuries were peak periods for wall builders like Irene Zegarelli's father, builders not of farm walls but of walls that were meant to decorate and to enhance, this type of wall—a wall born not of necessity but of affluence—had existed in New England and New York long before there were any Italian immigrants to build them.

These are the walls that prosperity brought to the New World, and they sprang up whenever New Englanders had a little extra money to put into their homes or communities. They are sometimes called "estate walls," though that term is perhaps best reserved for the walls of the very large estates built in Ceconi's time. This country's first walls of affluence were erected much earlier, in some cases not too long after the English and Dutch established their first settlements here.

Much of the stonework of the Philipsburg Manor in Tarrytown, New York, for example, dates back as far as the late 1600s. So does that of the Philipse Manor Hall located in Yonkers. Elsewhere, this second type of wall, a type that was much more carefully built than its farm counterpart, cropped up in different times for different reasons. In areas around Somers, New York, and Danbury and Redding, Connecticut, for example, some walls of affluence are the direct result of fortunes made from the nation's first circuses, which got their start in 1808 when Hachaliah Bailey acquired a female elephant, Old Bet, and began exhibiting her to farmers, cobblers, and wool spinners, thereby infecting the entire region with circus fever. On Martha's Vineyard, these walls have a somewhat different genesis, shadowing the growth of the whaling industry in the 1840s, and on the coast of Maine, some date back to the early

1800s when fortunes were made in granite quarrying and exporting apples to such faraway places as England.

In other parts of New England and New York, the reason for a particular wall might be less clear, especially today, after centuries of rising and falling fortunes. In one New England town, the residents, having suddenly found themselves prosperous because of an unexpected hike in beef prices, might have decided to erect a handsome wall around their cemetery or church using stone cut from a local quarry. Or a farmer, grown rich from selling lime or potash, might have contracted a day laborer to build a "fancy wall" around his newly renovated house.

But though walls of affluence did exist in colonial and early postcolonial times, by far the biggest boon to this second type of wall building was this

A handsome, quarried granite wall (note the pin-and-feathering marks) with a stone hitching post and mounting step.

country's industrial wealth, wealth that originated in the manufacturing and industrial revolution of the early nineteenth century. Originally, much of this wealth was concentrated in the cities of New York and New England, but it led to a spate of wall building in the countryside in the 1840s, when America's newly affluent began to abandon the cities for the country.

In the decades since the American Revolution, the cities of New York and New England had grown enormously—but so had their problems. In New York in the 1850s, walking down the street was a hazardous business. One could get mowed down by a marauding pig or stuck in the mud of an impassable street. Because of the lack of a safe and abundant water supply (in the early 1800s, most New Yorkers still obtained their water from private wells), everyone lived in fear of fire and the next bout of typhoid or cholera. In the first half of the nineteenth century, a disastrous series of droughts, fires, and epidemics made many New Yorkers desperate to leave.

Steamships and expanding railway lines made flight possible—at least for wealthier citizens. Along the Hudson River, where wealthy Dutch settlers had once built their handsome stone houses and walls, walls of affluence had always been a part of the landscape of this important waterway; estate wall building accelerated in 1849, when the New York Central and Hudson River Railroad established service from New York to as far away as Peekskill, and it reached its peak in the 1890s when the mansions of the so-called "Four Hundred," the families of New York's upper echelons of society, dotted the river. In Connecticut, nonagricultural wall building took off when New Yorkers made places like Greenwich, Connecticut, their summer and weekend resorts; it became even more widespread after 1848 when the construction of the New York, New Haven, and Hartford Railway turned Greenwich into a feasible daily commute. In southern Rhode Island, where most of the area's plantations had been dismantled in the decade before the American Revolution, estate wall building began again in earnest at the end of the nineteenth century when Newport became the fashionable place for New Yorkers to go during the hot summer months. And in the 1870s, after several artists had visited Bar Harbor, Maine, and made it widely known through their pictures, that remote locality was developed as a summer resort and filled with unusual examples of ornamental stone walls.

The walls that constituted this second kind of wall building in New York and New England were, for the most part, as different from the walls that the farmers of the area had built as a Rolls Royce is different from a Ford, or a thoroughbred from a Clydesdale. In building a farm wall, time and money were the critical, limiting factors. Farmers tried to make the best wall in the shortest amount of time; to do this they used the stones "as they lay," as they found them in the ground. Stone for estate walls, on the other hand, was almost always shaped, dressed, or faced to give the wall a finished, fancier look. Sometimes this stone was split or quarried using one of the methods available at the time. Gun powder, fire heating, and ice splitting were all methods used in the seventeenth and eighteenth centuries. Pin and feathering came in at the very end of the eighteenth century and remained the most widely used technique until the development of the pneumatic drill in the early 1900s.

Farmers also used some of these methods to get rid of large boulders in their fields and obtain stone for foundations, gate posts, and more, but whereas farm walls were built with stones that lay on the property, many walls of affluence were built using stone that had been quarried elsewhere, then transported to the site of the wall. Sometimes this quarried stone was "dimension stone," large blocks that had been "squared and trued." Other times, it might be rough, broken stone or grout—small pieces that were left over after the large pieces were quarried out. Near the old granite quarries of Blue Hill, Maine, there are several handsome, salt-and-pepper colored, grout walls, as well as some unusual walls built from paving stones—evidence of a paving-stone quarry nearby.

Wishing to avoid the farmer's spring ritual of fence mending, some estate owners opted to have their walls laid wet, with some kind of mortar holding the rocks together, rather than dry. The mortar in very early wet walls would have been slaked lime, an expensive and difficult-to-manufacture compound made from lime (produced through the heating of crushed shells) mixed with water and sand. Estate walls which were made during the nineteenth century and laid wet were probably put together using a mortar of natural cement, a compound made from limestone and screened sand which was far superior to its predecessor in terms of uniformity and durability. Today's wet walls are built with high-strength Portland cement.

Unfortunately for some of these property owners, especially those who had their walls built before the better kinds of mortar were available, the results were not always what they had hoped. A wet wall will indeed hold together well if it has a substantial foundation that extends below the frost line and if it is laid well with a properly prepared mortar. But should water ever get inside a wet wall and freeze (through pores in the mortar, for example), that wall will pull apart much faster than a dry wall—and it will be much more difficult to repair in the bargain. "A dry wall is a living wall," notes one contemporary

Many of the towns within commuting distance of New York City are known for their estate walls or walls of affluence. The roads of New Canaan, Connecticut, are lined with some particularly unusual and beautiful examples. This wall, which the illustrator calls "The Idaho potato wall," was built in the early 1900s out of stones that were, more than likely, dug up during excavation of the foundation of the house.

Another New Canaan wall, this time the six-foot-high dry wall in front of Philip Johnson's architecturally acclaimed "Glass House." People who live in glass houses should not throw stones, but they should, it seems, build tall, beautiful stone walls.

stone mason. "It moves and settles with the frosts. But if the frost gets to a mortared wall, it's going to crack and fall apart."

Another difference between walls of affluence and farm walls is one of ancestry. Unlike farm walls, most estate walls do not have an ancestry. For the most part, they were not the result of field clearing, the descendants of generations of walls made of brush, rails, and stumps. Rather, they sprang up *de novo* on the landscape. Their purpose, of course, was more aesthetic than functional. They were not built to enclose sheep or cattle, only the luxurious country and summer estates of America's newly emergent wealthy classes. Their purpose was to give scale to a house, to enhance its beauty, as well as to substantiate the wealth, position, and taste of its owners.

Estate walls also tended to be constructed, of course, not by their owners, but by jobbers or day laborers. At first, the men who did this work were those farmers and farm laborers who, in the course of building their own walls, found that they had a certain knack for laying stone, men like Asa Sheldon's father in Wilmington, Massachusetts. Later, in the nineteenth century, when agriculture became unprofitable for many New Englanders, farmers turned their knack for wall building into a livelihood, and a specialized class of stone masons and wall builders began to emerge. This class included people like John Matthews, better known as Waller John, who in the 1850s built many walls around Mount Kisco, New York. As time passed and the number of immigrants to this country swelled, the ranks of this occupation were suffused by laborers from other countries.

The Irish, who began immigrating in large numbers in the 1830s and 1840s following Ireland's devastating series of potato famines, were one of the first group of immigrants to take up this profession. Most Irish immigrants tended to congregate in the eastern seaport cities of Boston, New York, and Philadelphia, but some were recruited for work outside the cities: to lay railway track and to build, in the 1830s, the Croton Dam and Aqueduct, New York City's first (and desperately needed) reservoir system. Following the completion of this massive project, some of the ten thousand Irish laborers who had been involved remained in the Croton area and became independent building contractors and stone masons. In 1882, when New York City planners realized that the first Croton dam and reservoir wasn't adequate to meet the city's rapidly growing water needs and made plans to build a new and larger system, most of the contractors who submitted bids to build this new system were Irish. The labor for the new dam——or eighty percent of it——would be Italian.

Though the Italians were the second major group of nineteenth-century immigrants to leave their mark on the stone work of New England and New York, the mark they left turned out to be far more widespread and indelible than that of the Irish. For, as it became quickly apparent, many Italian immigrants had a far greater talent with stone. One Westchester writer has sug-

A third New Canaan wall incorporating large blocks of stone and a picket gate. Today, very few domesticated animals are enclosed or kept out by New England's stone walls, but these walls have become an important part of the habitat of numerous wild animals. The chipmunk here has probably several stored caches of nuts in this wall, which may also be home to many white-footed mice and the hunting ground of snakes, birds, weasels, and raccoons.

gested that stonework was in their blood. In his history of Westchester County, Alex Shoumatoff describes the estate walls of Westchester as having been laid by "Italian masons in whose blood the stacking of rock from the arid slopes of the Appenines into walls and dwellings had been running for centuries."

The Irish, too, had had centuries of experience with stone, so it is interesting that only the Italians acquired a reputation for this work in their adopted country. Both the typical Irish and Italian immigrant had been poor marginal farmers who, like their American counterparts, had separated their fields with stone. But in Italy, farmers had built walls for themselves because walls were the best solution to fencing in that treeless land. In Ireland, on the other hand, farmers had built walls because English landlords and settlers told them to. In the seventeenth century, the English, having outgrown their own small island, began to enclose large sections of Ireland for the purposes of commercial agriculture. Unfortunately for the Irish peasants, the land that they were ordered to fence had been their common grazing ground, and they found themselves increasingly shut off from any fertile land and from their former pastoral way of life.

Thus began a tumultuous relationship with walls that survives, in some form, even to this day and may explain why many Irish immigrants did not stay with wall building in this country. In the eighteenth century, secret societies like the Ribbonmen hacked down the hedges and leveled the walls of the English landlords. In the 1980s, when Alen MacWeeney and Richard Conniff began writing a book on Irish walls, they were surprised by the lack of interest and pride that the Irish felt towards what is certainly one of the most dominant features of the Irish landscape, and they concluded that "if the walls do not figure much in Irish folklore, the lingering sense of loss with them may be one important reason."

However the Irish regarded their walls, in 1892, outside of New York City, construction of the second Croton dam and reservoir began, and the timing, for both the contractors and the Italian immigrants, was almost perfect. In the 1890s, southern Italy, an area of the country where overpopulation was at its worst and where the soil was exhausted from centuries of intensive farming, was hit by a series of droughts and epidemics, and southern Italians started

A nineteenth-century quarry in which the stone masons are using the pin-and-feathering technique to split very large boulders into regular-dimension stone. Most of this stone would have been used for constructing buildings, bridges, and more, but some may have found its way into walls, especially walls built towards the end of the century when transportation was improved and the industrialization of New England and New York was creating a new affluent elite. Note that the holes for pin and feathering were made by men working in pairs with one man holding and turning the long steel drill or chisel as the other gave it blows with a striking hammer. Many of the laborers in the quarries of the nineteenth and early twentieth centuries were recent immigrants from Italy.

emigrating by the hundreds of thousands. At Ellis Island, many Italians just getting off the boat were met with offers of jobs. Some went north to work in marble quarries in Vermont; others went to Croton and the surrounding areas to work on the reservoir system. There an experienced stone mason or stone cutter was paid from $3 to $3.50 for a ten-hour day while unskilled laborers were paid less than half as much, $1.15 to $1.25. Skilled masons rented houses for themselves and their families in a settlement in the hills south of the dam, and the unskilled workers lived in a settlement at the base of the dam itself. It was called the Bowery, and the boardinghouse keepers there crowded as many men as possible into a single room——sometimes as many as 150 men into a room no more than 30 feet by 50 feet.

In addition to the many aqueducts, bridges, and dams which the pool of largely Italian labor built during the creation of New York's second reservoir system, the city's plan also called for the construction of what must be one of the world's longest dry stone walls, a wall almost eighty-four miles long. This is the stone wall that stands on the property line of the New York Board of Water Supply and runs around most of the New Croton Reservoir. It was built to protect the water supply from contamination by Westchester's previously large population of cattle, but now serves mainly as a source of amazement to the area's largely suburban population.

The wall *is* amazing. Besides being one of the longest stone walls in existence, it may also be one of the best built. Nearly one hundred years after its construction, much of it is still in excellent condition, which certainly has much to do with its enormous capping stones——most of them weighing at least one hundred pounds——which keep water and leaves out of the wall. Though I like to think that the city tapped the experience of generations of local farmers when it was deciding the specifications of the wall, this is definitely not a farm wall. It is much more carefully constructed, and it is built not of field stones but of large pieces of Fordham and Yonkers gneiss, the same materials used in building the reservoir's dams. For some sections of the wall, the narrow-gauge railroads which had been constructed in order to haul stone from the quarries to the dams also carried blasted stone to the wall builders, but in other areas, stone was carried in by teams of oxen. And in the *Minutes of the Aqueduct Commission,* at least one mention is made of a wall builders' camp, where some of the wall builders lived.

As with most of the walls of New England and New York, the complete story of this boundary wall has disappeared with the men who built it. Only its vaguest outlines can be pieced together by reading between the lines of those records from the period that remain accessible. An examination of the wall makes it obvious that it was required to be a double wall four feet high, with a carefully chinked filling of small stones, sides that slanted inwards at a slight angle, and large capping stones. The bids that various contractors submitted to the city to construct sections of this wall were recorded in the *Minutes of the Aqueduct Commission,* and they indicate that the wall was also required to "be trenched," meaning presumably that it had to have a foundation.

The firm of Culgin and Pace won the contract to build the "stone wall boundary fencing" around the Amawalk Reservoir section of the New Croton Reservoir with a bid of $96,200. But different firms were contracted for other sections. William J. Flanagan of Yonkers and then Katonah, New York, won the contract to build the walls around the reservoirs in Yorktown, New Castle, Bedford, North Salem, and Lewisboro, New York. He submitted a bid of seventy-four cents a linear foot, or a total of $96,000 for 130,000 linear feet. Today, to build just William Flanagan's section of the wall might well cost $10 million to $13 million.

Fear of contamination of the new water supply was, of course, the reason for the wall. It was also the reason why the city went to the considerable trouble of actually moving towns (house by house, cemetery by cemetery) which, like Katonah, New York, were not in the path of the proposed reservoir but were close enough to be deemed a threat. But, at the same time that the city was spending hundreds of thousands of dollars to keep Westchester's cattle from drinking from the public water supply, it was permitting a large settlement of dam laborers to live, cook, and bath in the area right below the dam. New Yorkers were horrified when in 1904, newspapers broke the story and showed photographs of Italians throwing refuse, watering their horses, and washing in the Croton river. Also pictured were piles of manure sitting on the banks of the river, piles described as being "roof-high." Physicians were quoted as advising their readers to boil their Croton River water.

And, of course, the reason why it was the city's responsibility to keep the cows out of the reservoir (and not the responsibility of the cows' owners) was New York's fencing laws, those anachronistic residuals from America's settlement days that ceded anyone's unfenced land into fair grazing ground for anyone else's cattle. Before the reservoirs could be fenced, the city tried to persuade cattle owners to keep their cows off the land, but with little success. The cattle owners, many of them angry at losing their farms to the encroaching reservoir, blatantly grazed their cows on property that the city had already laid claim to and, in many cases, paid for. George Nelson, the prosperous owner of three thousand acres and about a thousand head of cattle in Katonah, New York, repeatedly defied the city's request to keep his cattle off the city land and hid behind the fencing laws in doing so. He told newspaper reporters at the time that he would keep his cows "off the City land as soon as the City fences its reservoir."

In 1903, when it came time to fill the reservoirs, Nelson and fifty-three other farmers in the area refused to move. Nelson, a colorful character who wore a panama hat and diamond studs and rings even when he went out to survey his farms, was dubbed "King of the Squatters." In the end, one hundred deputies had to be sworn in to repossess the land and physically move sheep, horses, poultry, pigs, cows, furniture, and more to an area four miles outside the construction site. "This land should not be used any longer for farming and dairying," noted chief project engineer William Hill. His words would soon become reality. Today, there are fewer than 300 dairy cows in Westchester County, once the milk shed for New York City.

Once work on the Croton dam and reservoir system ("the world's largest masonry structure," the eighth Wonder of the World) was completed, the Italian laborers who had built it began to fan out into other parts of New York and New England taking their masonry skills with them. Gradually, they came to dominate the construction industry in many areas. In New York and some parts of New England, they also became well known as wall builders, skilled at laying both dry and wet walls and at re-laying old farm walls that years of frost heaves had tumbled down. For many years, theirs was not a well-paying job——during the Depression, wall builders were paid about fifty cents an hour——but more recently, the lot of the wall builder has improved dramatically, and a wall builder today can expect to earn at least twenty dollars an hour. Building a four-foot-high dry wall today could cost anywhere from forty to one hundred dollars a running foot, a far cry from the estimates received by the Board of Water Supply less than one hundred years ago.

Though the work of today's Italian American wall builders is generally much admired, it is so different in style from the crude walls that farmers once laid that to some New Englanders it looks out of place, entirely too neat. One

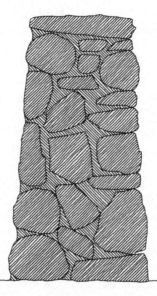

A cross section of a wall showing two different ways that stones can be laid up with mortar. On the left side, the traditional way of building a wet wall, with the mortar showing between the stones. On the right, a newer method of construction in which the mortar is hidden to give the wall the appearance of a dry wall.

Scarsdale historian expressed his opinion of the Italian style of building very bluntly when he berated the "Goddamned village of Scarsdale" for putting "an Italian mason on a wall that was over two hundred years old." The historian went on to complain that the mason "had squared off all the nice round stones."

An owner of an historic house in Bedford, New York (one of the very few houses in Bedford that was not burned during the Revolutionary War), recently contracted an Italian stone mason to build a wall and told him very explicitly that he wanted an old stone wall——not a new one. "What I got was an Italian wall" says the homeowner, "even though what I was asking for was something that would take a lot less time and a lot less care."

For their part, many Italian American stone masons view the farm walls of New England as little more than rock piles waiting to be laid. Italy is not a land littered with round, difficult-to-split glacial erratics, but rather a land where large blocks of rocks are easily obtained and carefully fitted walls easily made. I once asked a mason who was in the process of building a carefully chinked dry wall what he thought about as he drove by the old walls of New England. Did he mentally re-lay them and if so did it drive him crazy to do so? Yes, he said, he did mentally tidy up the walls as he drove along, but he tried very hard not to.

Another mason, a Spaniard named Manuel Cantarino who spends one-half of every year in New England laying walls and the other half with his family in Spain, talks about style from the point of view of the wall builder. Like many Italian wall builders, Cantarino's favorite kind of wall is a very tight fitting wall, the kind that is built in northern Spain where huge blocks of granite——perfect for that type of wall——are available. He doesn't like the stone that he has to build with here at all. The rocks are small and difficult to split, so he winds up having to use a lot of little stones to make the pieces fit. Cantarino, who is often asked to build a type of wet wall that looks like a dry wall——a wall in which the mortared joints are largely hidden——says that "sometimes you get very nervous building a wall like this. Let's say you have a hole but you can't find the right stone for it. The stones are too hard to break so maybe you have to put two stones together or maybe you have to make a new hole.

Whatever you do you have to do it quickly before the mortar hardens."

Spanish and Italian American wall builders are not the only ones who find it difficult to lay walls today the way the farmers laid them many years ago. Bill Merry, who has built walls on Martha's Vineyard since he was a boy, told an interviewer that he admires "rough-faced" walls and feels that "when you're building in an area that has rough-faced walls, it would look odd to do anything else."

"But," he admitted, "when I'm working on a rough-faced wall, I've got smooth-face in the back of my mind. That's something I'm trying to get rid of. When I have to repair a wall the way they had it, rough-faced, it takes me longer than it should."

This makes perfect sense, for Bill Merry is repairing these walls in an entirely different context from that in which they were laid. The walls were built in an agricultural context——one that put a premium on time and labor——but they are now being repaired in a time of affluence, when the premium is on aesthetics. And because they are so expensive to erect or to maintain, the stone walls of yesterday have become the walls of affluence of today. Today's farm enclosures——enclosures where time and money are still key factors——are made of entirely different materials, of barbed wire and electric fence.

11

THE WALL BUILDERS OF TODAY

LIKE the rocks they handle and lift and make into that pleasing thing we call a wall, the wall builders of today come in all different shapes and sizes. Some like Harvey Bumps and Dave Mason of Hartland and Starksboro, Vermont, are large and brawny and seem totally suited to the role of wall builder. Others like fifty-four-year-old Derek Owen are diminutive enough that you wonder how they could have found their way into this profession. Yet, as Owen has said, he can move a one-ton slab of granite by himself. And Hopkinton, New Hampshire, where he lives and works has a tradition of unusual wall builders. The wall around the town common was laid in the late 1940s by an eighty-year-old woman, Mrs. Margaret Emory, who thought it was only fitting that the common should have a wall so she built one.

"Give me a lever and I can move the world," Archimedes once said. Brawn isn't everything, wall builders will tell you. The secret to moving large rocks is not to use your back. "Roll it, slide it, or flip it over end to end," comments John Vivian, an amateur wall builder who has written extensively on the subject. "Use ramps or levers or sleds. And when you must use brute force, get behind and push with your legs. Bending double at the waist and heaving up on a rock is an invitation to a month of forced bed rest."

Even very careful wall builders wind up with their share of injuries. Manuel Cantarino sees a chiropractor for the sciatica that sometimes bothers him; and broken toes, pulled muscles, back problems, scrapes, and cuts all go with the terrain of laying walls. Though wall builders may come in different shapes and sizes, they all tend to have similiar hands—rough and calloused appendages that may or may not be missing a joint on a finger or two. A few of today's wall builders use a backhoe or forklift in their work, but for most of them, the task of wall building is as physically demanding as it was one hundred years ago.

The backgrounds of today's wall builders are as diverse as the walls they build. In southern New England and Westchester, New York, many of those laying walls today are the children or grandchildren of Italian immigrants. Others, like Cantarino, are recent immigrants themselves—from Spain, Alge-

Some of the tools of today's wall builders. From left to right: a stone mason's hammer, a small plain chisel, a point, and a larger chisel.

ria, Mexico, and other countries where the number of emigrants is high and where building with stone is commonly practiced.

In the northern states of New Hampshire, Vermont, and Maine, however, many of today's wall builders come out of a New England farming tradition; they learned their trade while working in the fields with their fathers. That's how Pete Clifford of North Pomfret, Vermont, began, by following behind his father's plow and carrying any stones turned up over to the fence line. "It didn't take me long to find out," Clifford, now deceased, once told an interviewer, "that if I didn't place the stone just right, it'd roll back onto my toes."

Chuck Hickey, Jr., of Pound Ridge, New York, was not a farmer but he also learned his trade from his father, a mason who was still building walls at the age of seventy-seven. Bill Merry also began building walls with his father, and for some of today's wall builders, a tradition of building walls in New England goes back in their families even farther, as far back as the late seventeenth and early eighteenth centuries. In South Kingston, Rhode Island, if anyone wants to restore or build a stone wall today, the first person they call is Robin Spears, a Narragansett Indian whose family has been building walls for generations.

Others came to wall building by less direct routes. Harvey Bumps took it up after he was laid off from a job building log homes. Dave Mason worked on road crews and in cheese factories and lumber mills before discovering at forty, when he was building a wall for himself, that he had a passion for this kind of work. Mitchell Posin of Martha's Vineyard married into farming and wall building. He became a wall builder when he and his wife decided to raise sheep on land in Chilmark that his wife's family had once farmed——some of the rockiest land in all of New England. Posin could have put up electric fencing to keep his sheep in, and dogs out, but he decided to repair the walls that were already there. By now, he has rebuilt more than three-quarters of a mile of his walls, a laborious process which has involved removing all of the soil and debris that has blown up against them over the years. Posin's walls are tall, between four and a half and five and a half feet (Posin, who is about six-feet tall, doesn't carry a yardstick but he aims for a height somewhere between the second and third button on his shirt) and of an unusual construction. Whereas most of the walls that go up today are double walls made of two thicknesses of stone, Posin builds single walls, walls just one rock thick. They are something like lace walls, but Posin insists that they aren't lace walls because the holes between the rocks aren't large——they have been carefully filled with shim or chink stones, stones which Posin calls "chalks" in deference to the Chinese.

As Posin or any of his peers will tell you, wall building is not for everyone. Only certain people find that they have the knack and the patience for it. Posin remembers that as a child, he excelled at three-dimensional puzzles. When Pete Clifford was asked what was required to be able to do the job, he said, "A person has to have a feel for stone, and has to be able to learn by observation. Some seem never to learn where to split a stone so that it will not shatter nor where to strike it with the hammer to get just so much off no matter how often they've seen it done. A very few get the idea easily and with practice the necessary skill."

Although wall building, always a labor-intensive way of making a fence, is now more expensive than ever, today's wall builders share a similar demand for their work (some are booked more than a year in advance, so some frustrated homeowners turn to wall building themselves) and a difficulty in obtaining the right stone at a reasonable price. Some of today's stone masons are content to work with newly quarried stone, but for many, especially those from a Yankee tradition, the only right stone is field stone. "We don't use any cut stone," says one New York stone mason. "It's all natural faces. Around this area it looks better."

"We don't like to show fresh edges," observes Derek Owen's nephew and partner Kevin Gardner. "We favor the older surfaces. The colors are better, more varied." Owen himself complains that freshly quarried stone tends to be covered with a fine grit that makes it very unpleasant to work with.

But with so few New England fields being plowed today, there is no new source for field stones, and most of the old ones are already tied up in walls. Wall builders buy old walls to take apart and use to make new ones, but not as readily as they used to. "Time was I could count on buying a stretch of old wall on a farm for the good stone in it," a Vermont wall builder has noted. "Not now. Often as not when I ask a farmer if he'll sell, he'll think a bit and then say 'Guess I won't.'"

Today, almost the only people selling old walls are developers who plan on demolishing them. Much of the field stone from these walls winds up in the hands of stone suppliers who charge $65 to $90 a ton for it. A ton is only enough stone for 15-18 cubic feet of wall—about three feet of a three-foot high wall.

At these prices, many wall builders are apt to forage for stone, searching the area where they intend to build. Some also blast and quarry for themselves. Pete Clifford knew many abandoned quarries in Vermont where he could still get good stone. Using just a stone mason's hammer and a hand tool called a point, he would drive the point in and start the stone leafing out in large, flat pieces. His biggest problem was getting his truck in so that he could cart the stone home.

Other, less scrupulous stone suppliers and wall builders are not above stealing an old wall. In June 1988, the *New York Times* ran an article entitled "Stealing the Stone Walls of Westchester" in which it was reported that thefts of stones—from the walls of homeowners, public roads, the reservoir system, even cemeteries—is rising as more and more people move into northern Westchester. "It comes down to money," Robert Gallo, a stone mason and contractor in the area was quoted as saying. "Years ago one could buy a cubic yard of field stone for $8 to $10 and now the price is upwards of $65. The stones are a temptation to someone who's looking for something he doesn't want to pay for."

Those who have had their walls pilfered face huge repair bills. "Someone could have part of his stone wall stolen and it could cost $15,000 or $20,000 to repair," Mr. Gallo noted. Nina Skolnick, a resident of Lewisboro, New York, who has watched the slow dismantling of a 500-foot-long, four-foot-high stone wall on her property, estimates that it will cost about $60,000 to replace it. "We're not talking about a petty theft," Mrs. Skolnick said, adding that though she prefers a dry wall, "I would never rebuild my wall now without using cement. I think that's about the only way you can keep it these days."

FINDING STONES IS only the first step of building a wall——and, of course, only part of its cost. Builders today will charge from $20 to $150 a running foot depending on the dimensions of a wall, the type of stone used, and whether or not there is to be a foundation. Their methods vary though certainly not as much as they might have one hundred and fifty years ago.

Some wall builders today still work by the adage that the more permanent you want a wall to be, the more of it you must bury underground. These men dig a substantial foundation for walls that they lay, a foundation that extends even below the frost line. As John Vivian suggests, "If you live in the Snow Belt and want the wall to be a permanent monument..., you should dig the foundation to below frost line. If you plan your walls as part of a building, particularly one that will house people or livestock, you *must* dig the foundation trench that deep." Most wall builders, however, dig their foundations only as far down as hard pan (or unbroken earth), and others lay their walls on level ground. Once a foundation is dug, the old-fashioned method is to lay the largest stones in the trench, but most builders today used crushed stone instead. As one observes, "if there had been crushed stone around two hundred years ago, you can bet they'd have been using it."

Although every wall builder agrees that when you're building a dry wall you have to obey the laws of physics and keep gravity on your side (meaning that you never place a rock in an upended or unstable position, such that it has a tendency to topple over), they don't always agree on how far to take this principle. Some masons argue that walls with a batter (walls that have a gradual, fifteen-degree slope inwards) are significantly more stable than walls with sides that run straight up and down, because "the batter lets gravity pull the wall in on itself as well as straight down on each individual stone." Others are not so sure. Derek Owen has made angled walls as well as walls with vertical sides, and he says he doesn't really know which one is best.

Some wall builders place their rocks so that they slope downwards and inwards, towards the midline of the wall. "As you build," notes Vivian, "try to imagine the effect of gravity pulling straight down on your wall. I like to have the rocks in all the courses angling down toward the center of the wall....Not always possible, but a help in aiding the wall to hold itself together." Many other wall builders, however, try to place their stones so that they lie as level as possible.

The important question of "through" or "tie" stones is one which receives surprisingly little mention these days. Through stones, as their name implies, are long flat stones which are placed every so often across the width of a double wall, thereby serving to bind all the stones together. Early commentators on wall building in this country rarely mentioned this, but some nineteenth-century authorities considered the placing of through stones to be "the most important part of the whole operation [of wall building]," without which "no wall, even if built of square blocks of hewn stone, will withstand the movement against which even the best foundation cannot entirely protect it." Builders were advised to place "tie rocks or 'thrufters' every six feet or so along the length of the wall so that they span the wall and give it stability," and in England, Scotland, and Wales even today, some wall-building contracts call for a proscribed number of through stones. In New England, however, through stones, like large capping stones (which incidentally serve the purpose of through stones, in addition to that of keeping out rain and debris), are difficult to come by, and many of the walls going up today seem to do with very few of them. The walls may still be tied together, but by rocks that do not span the entire width of the wall.

Today, when most stone walls are built for aesthetic reasons, their builders are necessarily concerned with rhythm, color, and balance. "Building a wall is sort of a patternistic balancing act," says Chris Gardner, another of Derek Owen's nephews and co-workers. "You want to keep a nice balance with large and small stones. That makes sense structurally and aesthetically."

Owen himself goes a step further and builds trademarks or signatures into his walls. His trademark, he says, is "Dotting the I's and crossing the T's," putting a round stone on top of a vertical stone, or a flat one on top of a vertical one. This is easier to do when building a wet wall. "You can pull more tricks with a wet wall than a dry wall," Owen admits. He is so good at building character into his walls that people now challenge him with stones. His nephew once found a stone that was shaped something like a half-eaten donut and presented it to Owen saying, "I bet you can't use that." The result was

Owen's totem-pole wall in which that unlikely, yellow stone features prominently. Because the stone's shape is also reminiscent of Owen's handlebar mustache, the wall-builder's wife refers to the wall as his self-portrait.

And what do wall builders see as the tricks of their trade? One on two and two on one is still as important as ever. "You've got to stay away from stack bonds," notes Owen, "from making a seam that runs down the wall. You can do this by putting one on two, two on one, one on three."

But there are others. "Once you pick a stone up, don't put it down again until you've found a place for it in the wall," I've heard many wall builders say. "If you do, it means twice as much work."

"The trick is to catalog the shapes of the stones in your mind, then match them with the shapes of the holes in the wall."

"Memorizing holes, that's what you're doing," says Kevin Gardner.

A rule of thumb for a wall builder in Maine is that every stone in a stone wall should touch nine others.

"Place wedge-shaped rocks with their thick side towards the wall's center so that they don't pop out with freezing and thawing," advises John Vivian.

What counts, adds Owen, is topping the wall with capping stones. "In the long haul," he notes, "a flat cap is better than a piece cap."

A mason in Vermont observes that "you want to get it so each stone can take the weight of the stone on top of it without changing position."

And Mitchell Posin saves himself hours of repairs by making it a rule never to walk his walls without a mallet so that he can knock any loose shims or chalks back into place.

Despite the physical hardships of wall building, few talk of leaving it to do anything else. It is obvious that solving these three-dimensional puzzles gives them a great amount of satisfaction. "My daughter says that I like rocks more than I like people," a Martha's Vineyard wall builder once said.

"When you're all done with a wall and you can look back, it feels good," observed another.

Several decades ago, Brooklin, Maine, resident John Clugh was drafted for a major league baseball team, but midway through the season he left to return home to his former occupation: wall building.

"And damn, but it is satisfying!" writes Vivian, who believes that "a stone wall is a work of art in its truest sense,... a creation of order out of chaos, of beauty from dross——as much an improvement on nature as may be accomplished by the hand of man." "A hard-won satisfaction to be sure," Vivian adds, "rock weighs a lot, goes up hard, and comes down harder."

Derek Owen standing in front of the 230-foot-long wall he calls his "Great Wall." Most of the wall was laid dry, but the section around the drain was mortared and in it Owen has "crossed his T's and dotted his I's," placed the rocks in the unusual, totem-pole like fashion that has become his trademark. "You can pull more tricks with a wet wall than a dry wall," the New Hampshire stone mason admits.

12

REDISCOVERING WALLS

"BEFORE I got interested in lichens," Mary Plant was saying as she peered through her magnifying lens at a particularly bright green specimen on a rock in an old farm wall in Stamford, Connecticut, "I used to read a lot of fiction. Each week, when the bookmobile came through, I would check out a new batch of novels. I would try to get Walt [her husband] to read them too, but he always had his nose in some science book. Now, I can't remember the last time I've read a novel. Now that I'm involved in this . . ." and Mary throws up her hands to show that what she means is the whole world, the natural world " . . . they just seem so trite."

Mary continued her examination of the lichen while I looked at the wall on which it was located. It was about five feet wide and made of two thicknesses of medium-sized field stones, separated by a jumble of small stones, suggesting that the land around the wall had once been cultivated and, probably, cultivated in a root crop or potatoes (for which it is advantageous to remove even the small stones). This type of wall, a rubble wall, is constructed on the principle that the filling between the outer layers of stone will shed water down and out through the sides so that it can't freeze inside and topple the wall. Judging from the condition of this one, that principle certainly seems to work. Crudely built as it looks, not a rock was lying on the ground; not one seemed on the verge of popping out. Moreover, one of the gardeners told me that it hadn't been touched in at least twenty years.

The wall, which is located on the grounds of the Bartlett Arboretum in Stamford, Connecticut, is also well-endowed with lichens—those strange, chimeric plants that are part photosynthesizing algae and part fungi—which was why I happened to be looking at it one wet day in June with Walter and Mary Plant, two amateur lichenologists. We had arranged to meet at the arboretum because Walter Plant, a retired high-school biology teacher, had said that we would find there a good diversity of lichens—and of walls. In 1900, the land had become the home and research grounds of Francis A. Bartlett, founder of the Bartlett Tree Company, but before that it had been the site of a pig farm. Before that, it had probably been used for subsistence farming. The walls reflect these changes, and in addition to farm walls like the one already mentioned, there are many decorative or garden walls built in Bartlett's time.

The day was an ideal one for looking at lichens. It had been raining off and on for weeks and was drizzling now as we walked from one wall to another. "You may never see them looking like this again," Walter Plant said, adding that during dry spells, lichens go into an almost dormant state in which their color and metabolism change dramatically. Mary Plant was telling me about the kinds of lichens one could expect to find on the rocks in walls and explaining that most lichens have a very distinct preference for either acidic rocks (granites and gneisses, for example) or basic rocks (limestones, as well as the mortar or cement that holds a wet wall together). Lichens come to inhabit rocks after they are exposed to air. And once one colony of lichens is established on a rock, it increases the likelihood of other colonies; it also produces the conditions necessary for the growth of mosses and, then, of ferns—all part of the slow, inexorable breakdown of rocks into soil.

The Plants and I had both arrived at our meeting with questions. Mine were about the kinds of lichens one might find on the stone walls of New England and whether these lichens could tell you anything about the age of a wall. These questions were part of a larger quest. Could the walls of New England's agricultural past speak to us, I wanted to know, and if so, what were the kinds of things that they could say about the land they enclosed, about when they were built and why. For their part, the Plants were curious about some of the unusual walls that they had seen in the woods of the arboretum. One in particular they had puzzled over: a small, circular enclosure that stood in the middle of four other, straight-sided enclosures. I couldn't be sure but thought that it sounded very much like an animal holding pen, a place to separate out animals for breeding, birthing, or treatment purposes.

We began to address my questions by looking at walls that we knew were built at very different times: the farm wall, a mortared garden wall built by Bartlett, and a new wall constructed in the last ten years. The difference in lichen growth was striking. While the wall of ten years had only one or two small colonies of lichens on it (and those may well have already been on rocks that were moved to make the wall), the older walls were covered with a beautiful green, blue, and gray array containing many examples of all three of the different lichen types: of crustose lichens (lichens so imbedded in the rocks that you can't pry them off), foliose lichens (lichens with a leaflike shape), and fructicose lichens (lichens with erect, soldierlike plant bodies). Lichens can colonize a rock at any time, the Plants told me, but the probability that they will have done so increases with time. Also, lichens are slow-growing plants (a growth rate of one centimeter a year is high and only found among certain of the faster-growing foliose lichens), so it takes a long time for these colonies to develop.

I was intrigued. Could this slow growth rate be used to date a wall? The Plants weren't sure; they had never thought about that, though they suspected that if any lichens would be useful in this regard it would be the crustose lichens, the slowest growing and least variable of all. Crustose lichens, I later found out, usually grow at a rate of about one millimeter per year or less, depending on factors such as the species type, climate, pollution (most lichens are extremely sensitive to pollution), and so on. Some have been observed for periods of up to ten years, during which time they have shown no increase in size. So if you see a crustose lichen on a rock measuring about five centimeters across (fifty millimeters), you can probably surmise it has been there for at least twenty-five years (lichen growth starts and is measured, not from edge to edge, but from a central point out to an edge) and probably much longer. If the colony is ten centimeters across (one hundred millimeters), it is at least fifty years old.

It gets more complicated when you try to apply this equation to rocks that are actually in walls. If you date (however approximately) a crustose lichen on a rock in a wall, you can only assume the same age for the wall if you know for certain that the lichen wasn't present on the rock when the wall was being built. And the only way you can know this is if you are dealing with a wall made of split or quarried stone. A field stone, farm wall covered with lichens is, of course, an old wall, but if you try to date it by any one lichen, you run into the possibility that that particular colony was already there when the wall was built.

Not a perfect way of dating walls, but then how could it be with all the

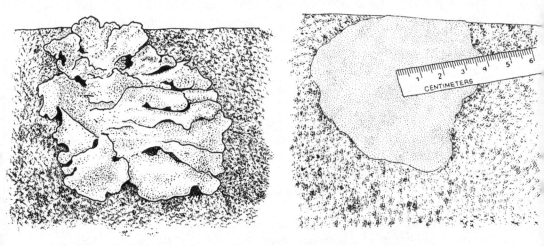

Two types of lichens commonly found on the stone walls of New England. While the foliose lichen has a three-dimensional, leaflike structure, the crustose lichen tends to be so embedded in the rock that it looks as if it has been painted on. Because crustose lichens grow at a rate of about one millimeter per year or less, they are of some use in dating a stone wall. A crustose lichen which measures five centimeters across has been growing for about twenty-five years. One that is ten centimeters across is about fifty years old.

variables that affect growth in a living thing? Lichens are best, perhaps, at adding one more piece to the puzzle of a wall, not at solving the entire thing. Some of the other things that help to date a wall—to teach, as author Annie Dillard might say, these stones to talk—have already been mentioned: documentation relating to walls (land deeds, fencing agreements, account books, and diaries), artifacts found in association with walls (ox shoes, coca-leaf vials, pipes, etc.) and, very importantly, tool marks.

When present on stones in a wall, tool marks can be the most immediately recognizable and accurate indicators of age. The first tools used for shaping stone in the New World did not, unfortunately, leave a readily discernible or datable mark. These were stone hammers, used throughout colonial and postcolonial times to shape rather than split stone. On the other hand, hand drilling (used with either pin-and-feathering or ice methods of splitting stone) did leave a very characteristic mark, an irregular groove five-eighths to three-quarters of an inch wide and three to five inches deep. Hand drilling and pin and feathering were techniques used extensively in the quarries of the late eighteenth century and most of the nineteenth century, but some farmers may have used them in their fields and backyard quarries long after that.

With the advent of steam, and then pneumatic engines, quarry owners, eager for a faster way of splitting stone, began to experiment with engine-powered drills. In 1868, a sixteen-pound, steam-powered rock hammer was manufactured for use in large quarries, but it soon proved to be more powerful than it was safe. Rock hammering was never widely adopted, so rocks with its signature, a peculiar, wedge-shaped pressure mark, are very rare. When the pneumatic drill was invented at the turn of the century, it quickly replaced previous methods. It, too, leaves a very characteristic mark, a long, regular groove or half-hole, often seven-eighths of an inch wide, which can be seen in rocks all along the roadsides and highways of New England and New York.

WALLS, THEN, ARE not as mute as one might think. They speak to us through these tool marks, the lichens on their stones, the artifacts buried in the earth around them, and the size of the rocks that they incorporate. They also speak in one other way: through the trees, shrubs, and vines growing on the land that they enclose and define.

Walls, as some naturalists and geographers have recently come to recognize, can tell us much more than the simple fact that the land on which they stand was at one time cleared and farmed. These objects are primary historical sources that can also help us understand what kinds of crops were grown and what kinds of animals were raised on a specific piece of land—the complexion and physiognomy of an early American farm.

Neil Jorgensen, a naturalist who wrote the *Sierra Club's Naturalist's Guide: Southern New England,* was one of the first to point this out. Jorgensen was puzzled by the patchiness of the woods of postagricultural New England, by the fact that the woods on one side of a wall, for instance, might consist only of black birch while those on the other side contain only white pine, and he hazarded that "the explanation for these differences is probably more than mere coincidence."

"Knowing something of the seed bed requirements of the various species, their desirability as livestock browse, or even whether the land on one side of a wall was abandoned before the other," observes Jorgensen, "may help you to make informed guesses by way of explanation." Chance, of course, has a great deal to do with what happens to any piece of land, so the naturalist cautions that "we can never predict with certainty what the succession pattern for a particular old field will be." But, he goes on to say, whether land was cultivated, pastured, or hayed has an important bearing on the forest that subsequently grows up on it.

The seeds of the red cedar, for example, almost always germinate in turf, so the presence of that tree is a sign that the land on which it is growing was once a grassy field. One is not likely, however, to see red cedars on land that has long been abandoned since cedars, like many sun-loving pioneer species, cannot compete with taller growing trees, such as hickories and oaks, and so they disappear in time from the postagricultural forest.

White pine is also a sun-loving species that grows best on land that was once a pasture, but because it is one of the tallest trees in the Northeast, it can survive for many years, even centuries. Livestock shun its seedlings (along with the seedlings of other conifers, red cedar, and ground juniper), so pines and cedars often appear in a pasture even before it is abandoned, thereby getting a head start on other species.

Land that was once a hay field might also wind up as a stand of white pine but it gets there by an entirely different route. The twice-yearly mowing of hay fields eliminated conifer seedlings (which cannot resprout from cut stems) but not the seedlings of many deciduous species and of shrubs (which can). According to Jorgensen, the open conditions of an abandoned hay field encourages the "vigorous growth of shrubs, sometimes producing a thick enough cover to slow down reforestation." Eventually, however, if the turf cover on the

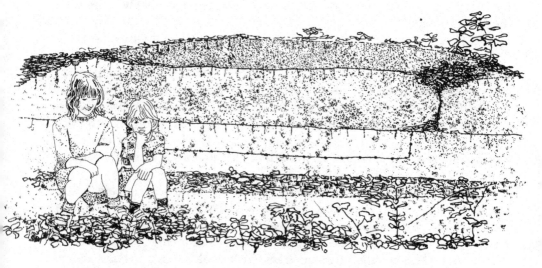

A backyard quarry from the 1800s. In parts of New England, it is not unusual to come across rock ledges and outcroppings which have been quarried on a small scale (using pin-and-feathering techniques) in order to provide foundation stones for nearby houses and barns.

field remains thick, the seeds of white pine and red cedar will germinate in it with the white pines eventually winning out over the cedars.

Land that was used for cultivation, on the other hand, results in a very different forest pattern. The bare ground of this land is an ideal seedbed for a wide variety of annual weeds which—because they require open and sunny spaces—do not last for long. They are replaced by perennial herbs such as goldenrod and wild aster and by such vines as wild grape and poison ivy. And where vines have taken hold, observes Jorgensen, "the vegetation often assumes a mosaic pattern that persists for many decades. Scattered trees that do manage to grow to maturity may remain and be separated from each other by a tangle of vines and other low vegetation."

Jorgensen is not the only one to look into the succession patterns of old farms. Recently, geographer Jane Dorney, who has written her master's thesis on the stone walls of Vermont's Green Mountains, examined the phenomena of the postagricultural forests in even greater detail. Dorney has been experimentally testing the seedbed requirements for different plant species in order to get a clearer idea of how a second-growth forest might be used to understand how the land was once farmed. Stone walls enter into her research not only as a way of directing her to different areas of land use but also because they too contain direct and indirect information about what transpired on the land they enclose.

Sometimes Dorney finds a stone enclosure with a row of aspen trees growing along the inside of the wall. Aspen only grow in sunny open spaces so she can surmise that the interiors of these walls were once open fields. She can also surmise that the land was once cultivated (if it had been in pasture, livestock would have eaten the aspen when they were small trees) and that these large trees started out as seedlings so close to the wall that they were missed by the plow.

Another puzzling pattern that Dorney sometimes sees is two stone enclosures standing side by side, the same height, but with very different widths. The walls of one of the enclosures are much thicker than the walls of the other but the additional width is entirely on the interior of the enclosure. Dorney interprets this as follows: the walls of both these enclosures were probably

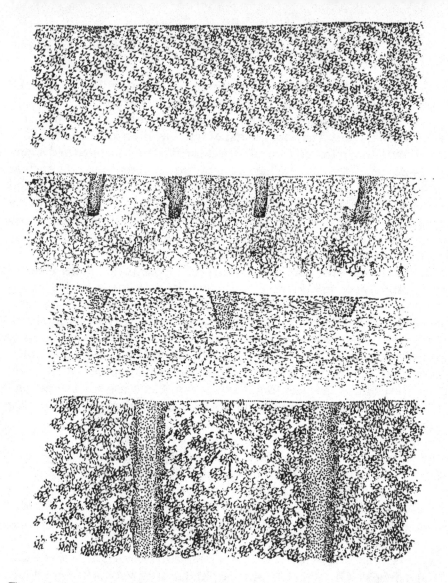

The marks left by various tools used to split stone. From top to bottom: flaking around the edge of a stone caused by blows from a stone hammer; the two-to-five-inch grooves left by pin and feathering; the wedge-shaped marks of the steam-powered, nineteenth-century rock hammer; and the long, uniform grooves of the modern pneumatic drill.

constructed at about the same time, but the land within one of them——the one with the wider walls——was much more intensely cultivated than the land within the other. Each year, the farmer picked additional stones out of the one field, and the easiest place for him to put them was up against the existing wall.

In northern Vermont, Dorney has also found the same pattern of small enclosures that exists all over New England and that contributed to the abandonment of many New England farms. Most of the enclosed fields she has examined are about five to ten acres in size (compare this to the twenty- to forty-acre fields of the early western states), but in Redding, Vermont, she has observed walled areas as small as one and two acres. Imbedded in these walls are, of course, the stones the glaciers left behind, but also centuries of New England tradition, the belief that small fields produce best.

No, stone walls are not mute after all. In recognition of this——and of the great aesthetic value of these once purely functional objects——at least a few New England towns have passed ordinances designed to protect their stone walls. The zoning by-laws of Chilmark state that "no moving, removing or otherwise altering an existing stone wall shall be allowed, other than for one driveway, in which case the stones from the opening wall shall be utilized on the property. Stone walls may be repaired." And in the town of Dublin, New Hampshire, it has been ruled that "no person shall deface, alter the location of, or remove any stone wall which was made for the purpose of making the boundary of, or which borders any road in the town of Dublin, except upon the written consent of the Board of Selectmen."

Stone walls, it seems, have not been entirely abandoned. The farmers who originally built them have moved on, but the walls are now attracting the attention of increasing numbers of historians, geographers, naturalists, and, of course, writers. Nor does their history stop at some point one hundred or so years ago when they ceased to function as either barriers or enclosures. A history which began during the Ice Age continues into the present; a new note to it is written every time that an old farm wall is dressed up and re-laid, every time that a load of capping stones is stolen for use in the construction of a new wall elsewhere.

In the years since this country was first farmed by Europeans, perception of field stones and the walls they were turned into has truly turned full circle. At different times, these durable objects have been seen as worthless impediments to cultivation, valuable fencing material, impediments to progress, and valuable aesthetic elements. Today, they are probably more prized than ever. And this new price on walls and on the field stone's head is bringing both new levels of appreciation and the dismantling of increasing numbers of old walls—another chapter in their complex, rich, and ironic history.

Red cedars in what was once an open field in New York state. Since the seeds of the red cedar almost always germinate in turf, the presence of this tree is a sure sign that the land on which it is growing was once a grassy field—either a hay field or a cow pasture. Cedars are also an indication that the land has not been abandoned for very long since, in the end, cedars, a sun-loving species, are unable to compete with such taller growing trees as white pines and hickories.

Selected References

Allyn, Charles. *The Battle of Groton Heights: A Collection of Narratives, Official Reports, Records, etc. of the Storming of Fort Griswold.* New London: 1882.

Alvin, Kenneth L. *The Observer's Book of Lichens.* London: Frederick Warne, 1977.

Andrews, Edward Deming. *The People Called Shakers.* New York: Oxford University Press, 1953.

Baird, Charles W. *Chronicle of a Border Town: History of Rye, 1660-1870.* New York: 1871. Harrison: Harbor Hill Books, 1974.

Banks, Charles Edward, M.D. *The History of Martha's Vineyard.* Edgartown: Dukes County Historical Society, 1966.

Bedford Historical Records. Bedford Hills: Town of Bedford, 1966-present.

Bell, Michael. *The Face of Connecticut: People, Geology, and the Land.* Hartford: State Geological and Natural History Survey of Connecticut, 1985.

Benes, Peter, ed. *The Farm.* Boston: Boston University, 1988.

Bidwell, Percy W. "The Agricultural Revolution in New England." *The American Historical Review* 26 (1921): 683-702.

Bidwell, Percy Wells, and Falconer, John I. *History of Agriculture in the Northern United States, 1620-1860.* Washington: Carnegie Institute, 1925; New York: Peter Smith, 1941.

Blakeman, Elisha D. *The Boy's Journal of Work. The Shaker Collection of the Western Reserve Historical Society.* VB-137 reel 36. Glen Rock, N.J.: Microfilming Corporation of America, 1977.

Bonney, Margaret Cole. *My Scituate* n.p., 1988.

Brewer, Priscilla, J. *Shaker Communities, Shaker Lives.* Hanover: University Press of New England, 1986.

The Colonial Laws of Massachusetts. Reprinted from the 1672 Edition by William H. Whitmore. Boston: Rockwell and Churchill, 1890.

Cronon, William. *Changes in the Land: Indians, Colonists, and the Ecology of New England*. New York: Hill and Wang—Farrar, Straus and Giroux, 1983.

D'Alvia, Mary Josephine. *The History of the New Croton Dam*. n.p., 1976.

Danhof, Clarence H. *Change in Agriculture in the Northern United States, 1820-1870*. Cambridge: Harvard University Press, 1969.

————."The Fencing Problem in the Eighteen-Fifties." *Agricultural History* 18 (1944): 168-186.

Deane, Samuel. *The New England Farmer: or Georgical Dictionary*. Worcester: Isaiah Thomas, 1790.

Delavan, Daniel. "A Description of the Town of North Salem." n.p. 1798.

Dwight, Timothy. *Travels in New England and New York*. 1821. Barbara Miller Solomon, ed. Cambridge: Belknap-Harvard University Press, 1969.

Farming in Mansfield. N.p.: Mansfield Historical Society, 1977.

Fell, Dr. Barry. *America B.C.* New York: Quadrangle-New York Times Books, 1976.

Ferrall, S. A. *A Ramble of Six Thousand Miles Through the United States of America*. London: Effingham Wilson, Royal Exchange, 1832.

Frost, Robert. *Complete Poems of Robert Frost*. New York: Holt, Rinehart and Winston, 1949.

Gardner, D. P. *Farmer's Dictionary: A Vocabulary and Compendium of Practical Farming*. New York: Harper and Brothers, 1846.

Goodrich, Samuel Griswold. *Recollections of a Lifetime*. New York: Miller, Orton and Mulligan, 1856.

Greeley, Horace. *What I Know of Farming*. New York: G.W. Carleton and Co., 1870

Hart, John Fraser, and E. Cotton Mather, "Fences and Farms." *Geographical Review* 44 (1954): 201-223.

————"The American Fence." *Landscape* 6 (1957): 4-9.

Hastings, Scott E., Jr., and Geraldine S. Ames. *The Vermont Farm Year in 1890*. Woodstock: Billings Farm and Museum, 1983.

Hawke, David Freeman. *Everyday Life in Early America*. New York: Harper and Row, 1988.

Holcombe, Harold G. "Stone Walls in Eastern Connecticut." *The Antiquarian* July 1959: 24-31.

Hoskins, W. G. *The Making of the English Landscape*. London: Hodder, 1955.

Hudson, Charles. *Southeastern Indians*. Knoxville: University of Tennessee Press, 1976.

Huntington, Gale. *An Introduction to Martha's Vineyard*. Edgartown: Dukes County Historical Society, 1969.

Hurt, R. Douglas. *Indian Agriculture in America: Prehistory to the Present*. Lawrence: University Press of Kansas, 1987.

Jay, Honorable John. "The Historic Memories of Westchester Co." Address given on the Anniversary Day of the Battle of White Plains, 1875.

Jorgensen, Neil. *A Sierra Club Naturalist's Guide: Southern New England*. San Francisco: Sierra Club Books, 1978.

Kalm, Peter. *The America of 1750; Peter Kalm's Travels In North America*. 1770. Adolph B. Benson, ed. New York: Wilson-Erickson, 1937.

Laws of the Royal Colony of New Jersey, 1770-1775. New Jersey Archives Series 3, Volume V. Trenton: Division of Archives and Records Management, 1986.

Leechman, Douglas. "Good Fences Make Good Neighbors." *Canadian Geographical Journal* 47 (1953): 218-235.

MacWeeney, Alen, and Richard Conniff. *Irish Walls*. New York: Stewart, Tabori and Chang, 1986.

Martin, George A. *Fences, Gates and Bridges: A Practical Manual*. New York: 1887. Brattleboro: Stephen Greene Press, 1974.

McManis, Douglas. *Colonial New England: A Historical Geography*. New York: Oxford University Press, 1975.

Mease, James, M.D. *A Geological Account of the United States*. Philadelphia: Birch and Small, 1807.

Melville, Herman. "Israel Potter: His Fifty Years of Exile." 1854. New York: Warner, 1974.

Meredith, Mamie. "The Nomenclature of American Pioneer Fences." *Southern Folklore Quarterly* June 15, 1951: 109-151.

Minutes of the Aqueduct Commission. New York: Gerry and Murray, 1883-1909.

Nash, John Adams. *The Progressive Farmer.* New York: C.M. Saxton, 1853.

Neudorfer, Giovanna. *Vermont's Stone Chambers: An Inquiry into Their Past.* Montpelier: Vermont Historical Society, 1980.

Noble, Allen G. *Wood, Brick and Stone: The North American Settlement Landscape.* Amherst: University of Massachusetts Press, 1984.

Nuquist, Andrew E. *Town Government in Vermont or "Making Democracy 'Democ.' "* Burlington: Government Research Center, University of Vermont, 1964.

Pearson, Haydn. "Stonewalls." *Vermont Life.* Spring, 1948: 50.

Rainsford-Hannay, Colonel F. *Dry Stone Walling.* London: Faber and Faber, 1957.

Read, John E. *Farming for Profit.* Philadelphia: J. C. McCurdy, 1884.

Roberts, Isaac Phillips. *The Farmstead.* New York: Macmillan, 1907.

Robinson, William F. *Abandoned New England: Its Hidden Ruins and Where to Find Them.* Boston: Little, Brown and Company, 1976.

Rollinson, William. *Lakeland Walls.* Clapham, England: Dalesman Books, 1969.

Russell, Howard S. *A Long, Deep Furrow: Three Centuries of Farming in New England.* Hanover: University Press of New England, 1982.

Salisbury, Neal. *Manitou and Providence: Indians, Europeans, and the Making of New England, 1500-1643.* New York: Oxford University Press, 1982.

Sheldon, Asa. *Yankee Drover: Being the Unpretending Life of Asa Sheldon, Farmer, Trader, and Working Man, 1788-1870.* Woburn: E.T. Moody, 1862. Hanover: University Press of New England, 1988.

Shoumatoff, Alex. *Westchester: Portrait of a County.* New York: Coward, McCann and Geoghegan, 1979.

Shurtleff, Nathaniel B., ed. *Records of the Governor and Company of the Massachusetts Bay in New England.* Vol. 1. Boston: William White, 1853.

Sloane, Eric. *Diary of an Early American Boy: Noah Blake, 1805.* New York: William Funk, 1962.

Starbuck, David R., and Margaret Supplee Smith. *Historical Survey of Canterbury Shaker Village.* Boston: Boston University, 1979.

Starr, F. Ratchford. *Farm Echoes*. New York: Orange Judd, 1881.

Smith, Wilbur, and Associates. *Cultural Resource Reconnaissance Study at Mystic Woods, Stonington, Connecticut*. Prepared for Kent Development. n.p., 1982.

"Statistics of Fences in the United States." *Report of the Commissioner of Agriculture for the Year 1871*. Washington: Government Printing Office, 1872.

Stephens, Henry. *The Book of the Farm*. Auburn: Alden, Beardsley and Company, 1852.

Stilgoe, John R. *The Common Landscape of America, 1580-1845*. New Haven: Yale University Press, 1982.

Teale, Edwin Way. *A Naturalist Buys an Old Farm*. New York: Dodd, Mead and Company, 1974.

Tennissen, Anthony C. *Nature of Earth Minerals*. Englewood Cliffs: Prentice-Hall, 1974.

Todd, Sereno Edwards. *The Young Farmer's Manual*. New York: Saxton, Barker and Company, 1860.

Town of Chilmark Zoning By-Laws. n.p., 1987.

Tree, Christina. *How New England Happened: The Modern Traveler's Guide to New England's Historical Past*. Boston: Little, Brown and Company, 1976.

Trento, Salvatore Michael. *The Search for Lost America: The Mysteries of the Stone Ruins of the United States*. Chicago: Contemporary Books, 1978.

van der Donck, Adriaen. *A Description of the New Netherlands*. 1655. Hon. Jeremiah Johnson, trans. Thomas F. O'Donnell, ed. Syracuse: Syracuse University Press, 1968.

Vivian, John. *Building Stone Walls*. Charlotte, Vermont: Garden Way, 1978.

Wagner, Jacqueline E. "The Training and Use of Oxen on the Farm in Central and Western New York." Thesis for M.A., State University of New York at Oneonta, 1970.

Waring, George E. *Book of the Farm*. Philadelphia: Porter and Coates, 1877.

Wiggins, Francis S. *The American Farmer's Instructor*. Philadelphia: O. Rogers, 1840.

Wilbour, Benjamin F. *Notes on Little Compton*. Ed. Carlton Brownell. Little Compton, Rhode Island: Little Compton Historical Society, 1970.

Wing, Bernice L. "A Vermont Sketchbook: Memories of a Vermont Quaker Farm." *Vermont History* 22 (1952).

Winthrop, John. *Winthrop Papers*. Vol. II, 1623-1630. Boston: Massachusetts Historical Society, 1931.

Woodward, Carl R. *Plantation in Yankeeland*. N.p.: Cocumscussoc Association, 1971.

Zelinsky, Wilbur. "Walls and Fences." *Landscape* 8 (1959): 14-20.

Also consulted but not cited individually are numerous agricultural journals from the nineteenth century (including *The Cultivator, The Farmer's Monthly Visitor, American Agriculturist, New England Farmer, The Farmer's Cabinet* and *Western Agriculturist*) and eighteenth- and nineteenth-century account books, land deeds, and fencing agreements located in the Dukes County Historical Society, the Fairfield Historical Society, the John Jay Homestead, the North Salem Historical Society, Old Sturbridge Village, Wenham Museum, and the Westchester County Historical Society.

INDEX